New York Saint Nicholas Society

Charter, Constitution, By-Laws and List of Members of the

Saint Nicholas Society

of the city of New-York - Vol. 2

New York Saint Nicholas Society

Charter, Constitution, By-Laws and List of Members of the Saint Nicholas Society *of the city of New-York - Vol. 2*

ISBN/EAN: 9783337409852

Printed in Europe, USA, Canada, Australia, Japan

Cover: Foto ©Andreas Hilbeck / pixelio.de

More available books at **www.hansebooks.com**

CHARTER,

CONSTITUTION AND BY-LAWS

OF THE

Saint Nicholas Society of the City of New-York

Founded February 28, 1835.
Incorporated April 17, 1841.

————◄◄►►————

NEW-YORK:
PRINTED BY ORDER OF THE SOCIETY.

———

1870.

Origin of the Society.

———•◆•——

AT A MEETING of several gentlemen, residents and natives of the city of New-York, held at Washington Hotel, on Saturday evening, February 14th, 1835, to consider the expediency of establishing a Society to be composed of old residents of the city of New-York and their descendants—

ABRAHAM BLOODGOOD, Esq., was called to the Chair, and WASHINGTON IRVING, Esq., appointed Secretary. The object of the meeting was briefly stated by Judge IRVING.

Doctor MANLEY offered the following Resolution :

Resolved, That it is expedient to form a New-York Society.

Which was unanimously adopted.

On motion of Mr. SCHERMERHORN, it was

Resolved, That a committee of five be appointed to prepare a Constitution and By-Laws for the Society, and that they report at the next meeting.

The Chair appointed Mr. PETER SCHERMERHORN, Judge IRVING, A. R. WYCKOFF, HAMILTON FISH, and Doctor MANLEY, as such Committee.

On motion, the Chairman and Secretary of the meeting were added to the Committee.

The meeting then adjourned, to meet again at the same place, on Saturday evening, February 21st.

ABM. BLOODGOOD.

WASHINGTON IRVING, *Secretary*.

At an adjourned meeting of citizens of New-York, held for the purpose of forming a Society, to be composed of the residents of the city of New-York and their descendants, at Washington Hotel, on Saturday evening, February 21st, 1835—

ABRAHAM BLOODGOOD, Esq., was called to the Chair, and WASHINGTON IRVING, Esq., appointed Secretary.

Mr. SCHERMERHORN presented a report from the committee of seven, appointed at the last meeting to prepare a Constitution for the Society.

Mr. MULLIGAN offered the following resolution, which was unanimously adopted.

> This Society shall be composed of those persons present at the adoption of the Constitution, who shall sign the same, and pay the sums thereby required, and of such other persons as shall be admitted members according to the provisions of the Constitution.

The Constitution reported by the Committee was then amended, by substituting, instead of the Monday in Easter week to be observed as the anniversary of the Society, "the sixth day of December in each year, unless that day fall on Sunday, in which case, the anniversary shall be held on the seventh."

On motion of OGDEN HOFFMAN, Esq., the Constitution, as amended, was adopted as the Constitution and

By-Laws of the Saint Nicholas Society of the City of New-York, and was referred back to the same Committee to classify the several parts as Constitution and as By-Laws.

OGDEN HOFFMAN, Esq., was, on motion, added to the Committee.

On motion, it was

Resolved, That the members present hand in their names to the Secretary, to be enrolled by him, and that such enrollment be considered as a subscription of the Constitution until such time as the Constitution is prepared to be signed by the members.

The following names were then handed in :—

(LIST OF NAMES.)

On motion, it was

Resolved, That a committee of five be appointed by the Chair to report at the next meeting, the names of suitable persons to be selected as officers of the Society, and that on the coming in of their report any member may be at liberty to nominate any other candidate than those reported.

The Chair appointed Judge IRVING, General LAIGHT, CORNELIUS HEYER, General JONES and ABRAHAM SCHERMERHORN, on this Committee.

On motion, the Society then adjourned, to meet again at the same place, on Saturday evening, February 28th, at half past seven o'clock.

ABM. BLOODGOOD.

WASHINGTON IRVING, *Sec'y.*

Chronicle.

A. D. 1835.

February 14th.—Meeting of Washington Irving and other gentlemen, at Washington Hotel, to consider the expediency of establishing a Society of old residents of the City of New-York and their descendants.

February 28th.—Adoption of the Constitution, and first election of officers.

December 7th.—First anniversary meeting at the City Hotel. By-Laws amended.

1836.

December 6th.—Second anniversary meeting at the City Hotel. The Secretary reported the names of two hundred and seventy members on the roll. Constitution and By-Laws amended.

1837.

December 6th.—Third anniversary meeting at Delmonico's. About one hundred and twenty members present.

1838.

December 6th.—Fourth anniversary meeting at the American Hotel. Permanent fund, $1,907.65 ; cash in bank, $637.23.

1839.

September 12*th.*—The Society adopts a flag, viz. : the original Dutch tricolor with the city arms in the centre. Flag procured at an expense of $51.93.

December 6*th.*—Fifth anniversary meeting at the American Hotel.

1840.

December 7*th.*—Anniversary meeting at the American Hotel. The Treasurer reported the permanent fund, $3,144.15 ; cash in bank $365.85.

1841.

April 17*th.*—The Legislature pass an Act incorporating "The Saint Nicholas Society of the City of New-York."

June 16*th.*—Resolution, and the appointment of a committee for the purpose of procuring "a room in a central situation for the laying of the foundation of a library and museum, as also for the meetings of the Society and use of its members."

December 6*th.*—Anniversary meeting at the American Hotel. About one hundred and forty members present.

1842.

March 10*th.*—Constitution and By-Laws amended.

December 6*th.*—Anniversary meeting at the American Hotel. The Secretary reported the actual number of members to be three hundred and twenty-three. Amendments to the Constitution and By-Laws ratified.

1843.

December 6*th.*—Anniversary meeting at the City Hotel. Constitution amended.

1844.

March 27*th.*—A committee, Samuel Jones as Chairman, recommended that at each Quarterly Meeting a lecture be delivered by such member as can be induced to address the Society, and that the stewards procure proper refreshments consistent with economy. That Tuesday in Easter week be the commencement of these celebrations.

It was resolved that the first meeting be held on Thursday in Easter week, April 11th, and that the price of tickets for the refreshments be set at one dollar.

April 11*th.*—First Paas Festival at the City Hotel. Constitution amended by fixing the second Monday of November as the time for the election of officers.

December 6*th.*—Anniversary meeting at the City Hotel.

1845.

March 13*th.*—The Society approves of the resolution of the Board of Officers as to the celebration of Paas on Thursday in Easter week, and that the price of tickets should not exceed two dollars ; and adopts the resolution of the Board as to the flag, the badge of the President and three new livery dresses.

March 27*th.*—Paas Festival at the City Hotel, at which Chief-Justice Jones delivered a lecture.

December 5th—The Society met at "The Stuyvesant Institute" in full force, and in the presence of the Presidents of the sister societies, wearing their official insignia, and of a very large assembly of ladies and gentlemen, J. De Peyster Ogden, Esq., delivered a lecture illustrative of the history and character of our Dutch ancestors.

December 6th.—Anniversary meeting at the City Hotel.

1846.

April 16th.—Paas Festival at the City Hotel.

December 4th.—Address before the Society by Rev. Thomas De Witt at the Dutch Church, Lafayette Place.

December 7th.—Anniversary meeting at the City Hotel.

1847.

April 8th.—Paas Festival at the City Hotel.

December 2d.—Address before the Society, at "The Tabernacle," by Charles F. Hoffman.

December 6th.—Anniversary meeting at the City Hotel. Constitution amended.

1848.

April 27th.—Paas Festival at the City Hotel.

December 1st—Address before the members of the Society, their families and friends, at the "New Assembly Rooms," 539 Broadway, by Hon. William A. Duer.

December 6th.—Anniversary meeting at the City Hotel.

1849.

April 12*th.*—Paas Festival at the City Hotel.　Price of tickets, $1.50.　A bill of $28 was subsequently paid for "extra eggs."

November 30*th.*—Anniversary address at the Chinese Buildings, by Rev. Thomas E. Vermilye.

December 6*th.*—Anniversary meeting at the American Hotel.　Permanent Fund, $6,647.90.　Cash in bank, $940.41.

1850.

April 4*th.*—Paas Festival at "Niblo's."

July 22*d.*—Special meeting of the Society upon the decease of Zachary Taylor, President of the United States.

December 3*d.*—Anniversary address, by William Betts, Esq., at the Chinese Building.

December 6*th.*—Anniversary meeting at Niblo's.

1851.

March 13*th.*—Adoption of the style of the Certificate of Membership.

April 24*th.*—Paas Festival at the Irving House.

June 12*th.*—Resolution for a new die of the Seal of the Society.

December 6*th.*—Anniversary meeting at the Astor House.

1852.

April 15*th.*—Paas Festival at the Astor House.

May 12*th.*—Special meeting to notice the arrival of

the Dutch frigate "Prins Van Orange," at this port. Committee appointed to provide a public dinner to be given to its Captain and Officers.

May 26th.—Grand banquet at the Astor House, on the occasion.

December 6th.—Anniversary meeting at the Astor House.

1853.

March 31st, Thursday.—Paas Festival at the Astor House.

December 6th.—Anniversary meeting at the City Hotel.

1854.

April 17th, Monday.—Paas Festival at the St. Nicholas Hotel.

December 6th.—Anniversary meeting at the St. Nicholas Hotel.

1855.

April 9th.—Paas Festival at the St. Nicholas Hotel.

December 6th.—Anniversary meeting at Delmonico's, corner Broadway and Chambers street.

1856.

March 24th.—Paas Festival at the Metropolitan Hotel.

December 6th.—Anniversary meeting at the Metropolitan Hotel.

1857.

April 13th.—Paas Festival at the St. Nicholas Hotel.

December 7th.—Anniversary meeting at the St. Nicholas Hotel.

1858.

April 5th.—Paas Festival at the St. Nicholas Hotel.

December 6th.—Anniversary meeting at the St. Nicholas Hotel.

1859.

April 25th.—Paas Festival at the St. Nicholas Hotel.

December 6th.—Anniversary meeting at the St. Nicholas Hotel.

1860.

April 9th.—Paas Festival at the St. Nicholas Hotel.

December 6th.—Anniversary meeting at the St. Nicholas Hotel.   Constitution and By-Laws amended.

1861.

April 1st.—Paas Festival at the St. Nicholas Hotel.

December 6th.—Anniversary celebrated at the Fifth Avenue Hotel.   Permanent Fund, 127 shares of the stock of the Bank of New-York, par value, $12,700. Cash balance in bank, $1,644.75.

1862.

April 21st.—Paas Festival at the St. Nicholas Hotel.

December 6th.—Anniversary meeting at Delmonico's.

1863.

April 6th.—Paas Festival at Delmonico's.
December 6th.—Anniversary meeting at Delmonico's.

1864.

March 28th.—Paas Festival at Delmonico's.
December 6th.—Anniversary celebration at Delmonico's.

1865.

The Paas Festival for this year was omitted, from respect for the memory of President Lincoln.

June 5th.—By resolution of a Special Meeting of May 16th, the festival of Pinckster was celebrated this day, by a supper at Delmonico's.

December 6th.—Anniversary Meeting at Delmonico's. Permanent Fund, $17,605. Cash balance in bank, $1,597.85.

1866.

April 2d.—Paas Festival at Delmonico's.
December 6th.—Anniversary meeting at Delmonico's.

1867.

April 22d.—Paas Festival at Delmonico's.
December 6th.—Anniversary Meeting at Delmonico's. Permanent Fund, $21,885. Cash balance in bank, $1,776.33.

2

1868.

April 13*th.*—Paas Festival at Delmonico's.

December 6*th.*—Anniversary Meeting at Delmonico's.

1869.

March 29*th.*—Paas Festival at Delmonico's.

December 4*th.*—Anniversary Address, by Hon. Jas. W. Beekman, at the Historical Society Building.

December 6*th.*—Anniversary Meeting at St. James Hotel. Permanent Fund, $23,820. Cash balance in bank, $1,895.32.

AN ACT

TO INCORPORATE THE

Saint Nicholas Society

OF THE

CITY OF NEW-YORK.

Passed April 17th, 1841.

The People of the State of New-York, represented in Senate and Assembly, do enact as follows :—

SECTION 1. Peter G. Stuyvesant, Washington Irving, George B. Rapelye, Egbert Benson, John Oothout, Abraham R. Lawrence, and Hamilton Fish, and such other persons as now are associated as the St. Nicholas Society of the City of New-York, or may hereafter become associated with them, are hereby constituted a body corporate, by the name of "THE ST. NICHOLAS SOCIETY OF THE CITY OF NEW-YORK."

SECTION 2. The objects of said Society are to afford pecuniary relief to indigent or reduced members and their widows and children ; to collect and preserve information respecting the history, settlement, manners, and such other matters as may relate thereto, of the City of New-York; and to promote social intercourse among its native citizens.

SECTION 3. The said Corporation shall have power to make or adopt a constitution and by-laws, rules and regulations for the admission of its members and their government; the election of its officers, and their duties; the suspending or expelling any of its members; and for the safe keeping and protection of its property and funds; and from time to time to alter or repeal such constitution, by-laws, rules, and regulations. The present officers shall hold their respective offices until others shall be chosen in their places.

SECTION 4. The said Corporation may purchase and hold any real or personal estate, but the annual income thereof shall not exceed five thousand dollars.

SECTION 5. The said Corporation shall possess the general powers, and be subject to the general restrictions and liabilities, prescribed in the third title of the eighteenth chapter of the first part of the Revised Statutes.

SECTION 6. The Legislature may, at any time, alter or repeal this Act.

SECTION 7. This Act shall take effect immediately.

STATE OF NEW-YORK, SECRETARY'S OFFICE.

I have compared the preceding with an original act of the Legislature of this State, on file in this office, and do certify that the same is a correct transcript therefrom, and of the whole of said original.

JOHN C. SPENCER,
Secretary of State.

ALBANY, *April* 19*th*, 1841.

Constitution.

Adopted at a meeting of this Society, February 28th, A. D. 1835.
Amendments Adopted December 6th, A. D. 1860.
"   "   March 19th, A. D. 1863.

ARTICLE I.

OF THE NAME OF THE SOCIETY.

SECTION 1. The name of this Society shall be "THE ST. NICHOLAS SOCIETY OF THE CITY OF NEW-YORK," and its objects shall be to afford pecuniary relief to indigent or reduced members of this Society, and their widows and children ; to collect and preserve information respecting the history, settlement, manners, &c., of the City of New-York ; and to promote social intercourse among its native citizens.

ARTICLE II.

OF MEMBERS.

SECTION 1. Any person of full age, in respectable standing in society, of good moral character, who was a native or resident of the City or State of New-York prior to the year 1785, or who is the descendant of any such native or resident, or who is a descendant of a member of this Society, shall be eligible as a member.

SECTION 2. Candidates for admission must be proposed at either a stated or special meeting, whether there be a quorum or not, by a member, who shall state in writing the name of the candidate, his profession or occupation, his place of residence, and that he is known to have the requisites for admission. At the next succeeding meeting of the Board of Officers, or on such day thereafter as they may think proper, they shall proceed to ballot for his admission; and if there be three-fourths of the votes of the officers present, in his favor, he shall be elected.

SECTION 3. Each member shall, immediately on his election, sign the Constitution, and pay to the Treasurer his initiation fee, and the annual dues for the current year; and shall not take his seat as a member until he shall have complied with the requisitions of this section.

SECTION 4. The initiation fee shall be five dollars, and each member shall annually pay the sum of two dollars (in advance for the ensuing year) on the anniversary meeting in each year.

SECTION 5. The payment at one time of twenty-five dollars or more shall constitute a life member; and the member so paying shall be exempt from the future payment of the annual dues.

SECTION 6. If any member neglect or refuse to pay his annual dues for the space of one year after the same shall become due, he shall be considered to have resigned his membership; and his name shall be stricken from the roll of the Society, unless some good reason for such neglect or refusal be presented to the Board of Officers; in which case the said Board may by resolution continue him as a member.

SECTION 7. Any member wishing to resign, shall tender his resignation in writing, which may be accepted, provided the amount of dues (if any) for which said member may be in arrears, shall be then paid up.

ARTICLE III.

OF THE OFFICERS OF THE SOCIETY.

SECTION 1. There shall be annually elected, on the second Monday of November, at a special meeting to be called for such purpose, from among the members of this Society, a President, a First, a Second, a Third, and a Fourth Vice-President, twelve Managers, a Treasurer, a Secretary, and an Assistant Secretary, who shall constitute the "Board of Officers." There shall also be elected at the same time, two Chaplains, two Physicians, and two Consulting Physicians.

SECTION 2. The election shall be by ballot, and a plurality of votes shall constitute a choice.

SECTION 3. The officers so elected shall be installed and shall enter upon the duties of their respective offices on the anniversary meeting next ensuing.

SECTION 4. The President shall, when he is present, preside at all meetings of the Society, preserve order, put the question, and declare the decision. He, in conjunction with one of the Vice-Presidents, may call special meetings of the Society when they shall judge proper, and he shall call them when required by the Board of Officers, or when requested in writing by any nine members, specifying in such request the object for which such meeting is desired. He shall appoint the time and place of all meetings, and shall sign orders on the Treasurer from the Board of Officers.

SECTION 5. The Vice-Presidents shall assist the President in presiding at the meetings. The duties specified in the preceding section, shall, in case of the inability to act of the President, by reason of his absence or sickness, devolve on the first Vice-President; and in the absence or sickness of both, on the second Vice-President; and so on, according to rank; only that, in regard to signing orders on the Treasurer, each shall have equal powers with the President.

SECTION 6. The Managers shall constitute a Board for dispensing the Society's bounty, agreeably to the regulations and restrictions prescribed in this Constitution, or by the laws and resolves of this Society; and, for this purpose, they shall meet at least once a month in summer, and twice a month in winter; and five shall be necessary to form a quorum. At their meetings only they shall decide on the application of claimants, and if a majority of those present shall consent to grant relief, they shall recommend them, in writing, to the President and Vice-Presidents, either of whom is authorized to draw on the Treasurer for the sum specified in the recommendation of the Managers ; provided that no more than twelve dollars be given to any one person in one year, except as provided in Article VI., Section 1, of this Constitution, or unless otherwise determined at a meeting of the Society ; and provided also, that the whole sum thus dispensed by the Managers and by the Society in one year, do not exceed the revenue of the Society for that year, arising from the interest on the permanent fund, (hereafter mentioned,) and from the annual dues. The Managers shall likewise recommend to the attention of the Chap-lains and Physicians such persons as they suppose might be benefitted by their assistance.

SECTION 7. The Treasurer shall have the custody of the money and other property of the Society. He shall keep regular accounts of all receipts and disbursements, in suitable books provided for that purpose, which shall be open at all reasonable times to the inspection of the members. He shall keep an account of the fees and dues that accrue, and shall appoint a proper and discreet person to collect the same, and shall allow such person a reasonable compensation therefor. He shall, at least once in every three months, report to the Board of Officers the names of the members whose dues remain unpaid, and the amount they respectively owe—specifying those whose dues have been in arrear more than a year. He shall preserve vouchers for all disbursements. He shall enter on his books each sum paid by him in consequence of the recommendation of the Board of Managers, the name of the President or the Vice-President who signed the order, and the name of the person to whom the money was paid. He shall at each quarterly meeting present an abstract of his accounts, stating the sum received and expended during the last quarter; and likewise the whole amount received and expended since the previous anniversary festival, specifying the amount of the permanent fund, and amount of cash in hand, and what may become due before the next meeting of the Society, that they may, if they think proper, take order for the disposition thereof.

SECTION 8. The Secretary shall have the custody of all the records and journals of the Society, and shall make a regular entry of all the proceedings at each meeting. He shall keep a roll of the members. He shall give notice in the newspapers of all meetings, whether stated or special. He shall, under the direction of the Board of Officers, erase from the list of members the names of all such persons as shall by the terms of the Constitution have forfeited their title to membership, making report thereof at the next meeting of the Society.

SECTION 9. In the absence of the Secretary, the duties specified by the last preceding section shall devolve on the Assistant Secretary, whose duty it shall be to assist the Secretary when present.

SECTION 10. The Chaplains shall perform the religious duties at the meetings of the Society, and shall by their counsel and advice promote harmony and good-will among the members. They shall also visit such sick and distressed persons as may be recommended to their attention by the Managers.

SECTION 11. The Physicians shall give advice and assistance to such sick or maimed person as may be committed to their care by the Managers.

SECTION 12. In case of the death, resignation, or removal of any of the officers before the end of the year for which they were elected, the Society may, at any subsequent meeting, choose others in their room, in the mode prescribed in Section 2, of this Article, to serve for the remainder of the term for which such officers were elected.

SECTION 13. The Board of Officers shall meet regularly on the Monday immediately preceding each quarterly meeting. Special meetings may be called by the Secretary, under the direction of the President, or of the Vice-President acting in his stead, or of any three members of the Board of Officers. In addition to the duties conferred upon the Board by this Constitution, they shall likewise execute all such business as may from time to time be committed to them by any law or resolve of the Society; and they shall report their proceedings at every stated meeting of the Society. The presence of at least seven members shall be necessary for the transaction of business. They may, in their discretion, appoint a Sergeant-at-Arms, with such powers, and subject to such duties, as they may deem proper; and may allow him such compensation as they shall think reasonable.

ARTICLE IV.

OF COMMITTEES.

SECTION 1. The Committee of Finance shall consist of the President, the Vice-Presidents, and Treasurer; the President shall be Chairman of the Committee. They shall have the management of the permanent fund, and shall direct its investment. All funds and money belonging to the Society shall stand in the name of "The St. Nicholas Society of the City of New-York." The Committee shall, when moneys are to be disbursed from the permanent fund, or any amount transferred therefrom by resolution of the Society, give an order, in writing to the Treasurer, for such disbursement or transfer. They shall have power to sell out stocks or other securities belonging to the Society, and to reinvest the same. They shall report their proceedings at each quarterly meeting.

SECTION 2. There shall be appointed annually, at the meeting when the officers of the Society are elected, a Committee of Accounts, consisting of five members, not being officers, whose duty it shall be to examine the books and accounts and vouchers of the Treasurer, and to examine the proceedings of the Committee of Finance and of the Managers, and to report thereon to the Society at its next meeting.

SECTION 3. There shall annually be appointed, at the meeting when the officers of the Society are elected, a Committee of Instalment, consisting of two members, who shall, on the anniversary festival, present and install the officers elected for the ensuing year.

SECTION 4. There shall annually be elected by the Society, by ballot, at the meeting when the officers are elected, a committee of seven, as Stewards of the Society, for the ensuing year, whose duty it shall be to take charge of the general detail of the anniversary celebration, as shall be prescribed by the By-Laws, or by a resolution of the Society.

SECTION 5. All Committees (special as well as standing) whose appointment is not otherwise directed by the Constitution or By-Laws, or a resolution of the Society, shall be nominated by the presiding officer, and confirmed by the Society.

ARTICLE V.

OF THE FUNDS.

SECTION 1. All sums received as initiation fees, donations, bequests, &c., and all sums paid by life members, shall be invested under the direction of the committee of Finance as a Permanent Fund, to be loaned out at interest, or invested in stocks, or public funds. And if at any time the interest arising from the Permanent Fund, together with the amount received from the annual dues, be more than the exigencies of the poor and the current expenses of the Society require, the

3

surplus shall be carried to the Permanent Fund. In like manner, if the Stewards shall at any time receive more money than is required for the expenses of the anniversary festival, the surplus shall be paid over to the Treasurer, and be carried to the Permanent Fund.

SECTION 2. No money shall be transferred from the Permanent Fund, except by a resolution of the Society at a stated meeting, at which there shall be present at least one hundred members, three-fourths of whom shall vote in favor of such resolution.

SECTION 3. All such sums as arise from the annual dues of members, and from the interest or income of the Permanent Fund, shall constitute a fund, to be called the Charity and Expense Fund, from which all the debts of the Society shall be paid, and the charities disbursed. But if the said fund shall exceed the amount of expenses and of charities distributed, the surplus shall be annually carried to the Permanent Fund, according to the provisions of Section 1, of this Article of the Constitution.

ARTICLE VI.

OF THE PERSONS TO WHOM CHARITABLE DONATIONS MAY BE MADE.

SECTION 1. The widow and children of a deceased member shall (if so determined by the Board of Managers) be entitled for five successive years to an annuity from the funds of the Society, to the full amount of the moneys which the deceased member shall have actually paid into the Treasury, payable in such manner, and to such persons, as the said Board of Managers shall direct; provided, however, that said annuity shall in no case be paid to a widow of a member after she shall have married again, nor to children after they shall have attained the age of fourteen years.

SECTION 2. None shall be objects of the Society's bounty (except as provided in the preceding section) but such members thereof as shall become indigent, and children of a member of this Society.

ARTICLE VII.

OF MEETINGS.

SECTION 1. The Society shall hold four stated quarterly meetings in each year, on such days as shall be determined by the By-Laws.

SECTION 2. Special meetings may be called as provided in Section 4, Article III. of this Constitution. Special meetings shall be competent for the transaction of any business which may come before them, except questions touching a transfer of the Permanent Fund of the Society, and except also such other business as by this Constitution, or the By-Laws, may be confined to stated meetings.

SECTION 3. As the benevolent and charitable objects of this Society will be greatly promoted by a social intercourse among its members, the Society shall celebrate its anniversary by a dinner, on the sixth day of December in each year, unless that day fall on Sunday, in which case the anniversary shall be held on the following day, and the Society may at any stated meeting provide for other festivities.

SECTION 4. All the meetings of the Society shall be held at such hour and place as the President, or person acting as President for the time being, shall appoint.

SECTION 5. A quorum for the dispatch of business, except in cases where a larger number may be required for any special act, by any article of the Constitution, shall consist of such number of members as shall be prescribed by the By-Laws; but any number of members present at the time appointed for a stated meeting, may from time to time adjourn such stated meeting.

SECTION 6. The names of all members voting in favor of, or against any resolution, shall be entered on the minutes, if required by one-fourth of the members present at any meeting.

ARTICLE VIII.

ON THE MODE OF ALTERING THE CONSTITUTION OF THE SOCIETY.

SECTION 1. No alteration, repeal or amendment of any part of this Constitution shall take place unless the proposition for such alteration, repeal, or amendment shall have been made at a previous stated meeting; and such proposition shall not take effect unless there are present at least forty members, three-fourths of whom shall vote in the affirmative, and the votes on such question shall be recorded by the Secretary, if required by five members present.

SECTION 2. The By-Laws of this Society may be altered, repealed, or amended, either at a stated meeting, or at a special meeting, when called for the object of making such alteration, such object being expressed in the notice of said special meeting. The proposition for such alteration, repeal, or amendment, must have been made at a previous meeting.

By-Laws.

SECTION 1. The stated meetings of this Society shall be held on the first Thursday in March, June, and September, and on the Thursday next before the anniversary, in each year.

SECTION 2. The Secretary shall give at least two days' notice, through the public newspapers, of the time and place of all meetings, whether special or stated.

SECTION 3. At special meetings, the consent of two-thirds of the members present shall be necessary to constitute a vote.

SECTION 4. Fifteen members shall be necessary to constitute a quorum, except in cases where a larger number may be required by the Constitution or By-Laws, for any special act.

SECTION 5. At each meeting of the Society, immediately after the presiding officer shall have taken the chair, the minutes of the previous meeting shall be read by the Secretary, and passed upon by the Society; the next business in order shall be reports of officers and committees; then resolutions offered; then proposal of candidates.

SECTION 6. Any member having observations to make, or resolutions to propose, shall rise in his place and address the Chair; and all resolutions shall be submitted in writing, and handed to the Secretary, and shall be by him entered on the minutes.

SECTION 7. In all cases of candidates for admission, the member proposing a candidate shall state, in writing under his own signature, in the " Book of Proposals," the name of the person proposed, his occupation and residence; also, the name of the ancestor, who was a native or resident of the City or State of New-York, prior to the year 1785, or who has been a member of this Society; and the degree of relation between the candidate and such ancestor; and also, all other qualifications required by the Constitution ; and no name shall be considered in nomination, unless the proposal be submitted to a meeting of the Society in the manner required by this section.

SECTION 8. When a candidate is proposed for admission, any member present may state any facts within his knowledge, respecting the qualifications of the candidate so proposed.

SECTION 9. The Stewards shall select the place of meeting for, and shall provide the anniversary dinner ; shall stipulate the price, and issue tickets therefor ; and, in conjunction with the President and Vice-Presidents, shall prepare the toasts, and sign and give invitation cards to the dinner.

SECTION 10. No topic connected with the party politics of the day shall ever be discussed at the meetings of this Society.

List of Officers.

Officers for the Year 1835.	Officers for the Year 1836.
President, PETER G. STUYVESANT.	*President,* PETER G. STUYVESANT.
1st Vice-President, ABRAHAM BLOODGOOD,	*1st Vice-President,* ABRAHAM BLOODGOOD.
2d Vice-President, WASHINGTON IRVING.	*2d Vice-President,* WASHINGTON IRVING.
3d Vice-President, GULIAN C. VERPLANCK.	*3d Vice-President,* GULIAN C. VERPLANCK.
4th Vice-President, PETER SCHERMERHORN.	*4th Vice-President,* PETER SCHERMERHORN.
Treasurer, JOHN OOTHOUT.	*Treasurer,* JOHN OOTHOUT.
Secretary, HAMILTON FISH.	*Secretary,* HAMILTON FISH.
Assistant Secretary, WM. A. LAWRENCE.	*Assistant Secretary,* WM. A. LAWRENCE.

1835

Managers,
CORNELIUS HEYER,
ROBERT BENSON,
THOMAS R. MERCEIN,
ABRAHAM ASTEN,
JOHN W. MULLIGAN,
JAMES L. BRINCKERHOFF,
JAMES R. MANLEY,
ALEX. R. WYCKOFF,
JEROMUS JOHNSON,
DANIEL E. TYLEE,
CHARLES GRAHAM,
JOHN LEVERIDGE.

Chaplains,
RT. REV. BENJ. T. ONDERDONK,
REV. ROBERT M'CARTEE.

Physicians,
WILLIAM H. HOBART,
EDWARD G. LUDLOW,

Consulting Physicians,
HUGH M'LEAN,
JOHN W. FRANCIS.

Stewards,
ABM. SCHERMERHORN,
DANIEL B. DASH,
JAMES I. JONES,
OGDEN HOFFMAN,
ROBERT RAY,
CHARLES H. HAMMOND,
JACOB R. LE ROY.

1836

Managers,
CORNELIUS HEYER,
ROBERT BENSON,
THOMAS R. MERCEIN,
ABRAHAM ASTEN,
JOHN W. MULLIGAN,
JAMES L. BRINCKERHOFF,
JAMES R. MANLEY, .
ALEX. R. WYCKOFF,
JEROMUS JOHNSON,
DANIEL E. TYLEE,
CHARLES GRAHAM,
JOHN LEVERIDGE.

Chaplains,
RT. REV. BENJ. T. ONDERDONK,
REV. ROBERT M'CARTEE.

Physicians,
WILLIAM H. HOBART,
EDWARD G. LUDLOW.

Consulting Physicians,
HUGH M'LEAN,
JOHN W. FRANCIS.

Stewards,
OGDEN HOFFMAN,
JACOB R. LE ROY,
DANIEL B. DASH,
ROBERT RAY,
EGBERT BENSON,
AUGUSTUS FLEMING,
CHARLES H. HAMMOND.

Officers for the Year 1837.

President,
GULIAN C. VERPLANCK.

1st Vice-President,
WASHINGTON IRVING.

2d Vice-President,
PETER SCHERMERHORN.

3d Vice-President,
CORNELIUS HEYER.

4th Vice-President,
EGBERT BENSON.

Treasurer,
JOHN OOTHOUT.

Secretary,
HAMILTON FISH.

Assistant Secretary,
WM. A. LAWRENCE.

Managers,
JAMES R. MANLEY.
THOMAS R. MERCEIN,
ABRAHAM ASTEN,
JOHN W. MULLIGAN,
JAMES L. BRINCKERHOFF,
ABEL T. ANDERSON,
ROBERT BENSON,
JEROMUS JOHNSON,
DANIEL E. TYLEE,
CHARLES GRAHAM,
JOHN LEVERIDGE,
GEORGE B. RAPELYE.

Chaplains,
RT. REV. BENJ. T. ONDERDONK,
REV. ROBERT M'CARTEE.

Physicians,
WILLIAM H. HOBART,
EDWARD G. LUDLOW.

Consulting Physicians,
HUGH M'LEAN,
JOHN W. FRANCIS.

Stewards,
OGDEN HOFFMAN,
SAMUEL SWARTWOUT,
DAVID C. COLDEN,
ALEX. R. WYCKOFF,
ANTHONY J. BLEECKER,
JONATHAN NATHAN,
JAMES BOWEN.

Officers for the Year 1838.

President,
GULIAN C. VERPLANCK.

1st Vice-President,
WASHINGTON IRVING.

2d Vice-President,
PETER SCHERMERHORN.

3d Vice-President,
CORNELIUS HEYER.

4th Vice-President,
EGBERT BENSON.

Treasurer,
JOHN OOTHOUT.

Secretary,
HAMILTON FISH.

Assistant-Secretary,
WM. A. LAWRENCE.

Managers,
JAMES R. MANLEY,
THOMAS R. MERCEIN,
ABRAHAM ASTEN,
CHARLES GRAHAM,
ABEL T. ANDERSON,
HENRY BEECKMAN,
ROBERT BENSON,
JEROMUS JOHNSON,
JOHN W. MULLIGAN,
JOHN LEVERIDGE,
GEORGE B. RAPELYE,
WILLIAM J. VAN WAGENEN.

Chaplain,
RT. REV. BENJ. T. ONDERDONK.

Physicians,
WILLIAM H. HOBART,
JOHN D. OGDEN.

Consulting Physicians,
JOHN W. FRANCIS,
HUGH M'LEAN.

Stewards,
ALEX. R. WYCKOFF,
DAVID C. COLDEN,
JAMES BOWEN,
ANTHONY J. BLEECKER,
JONATHAN NATHAN,
JOHN A. KING,
JAMES J. JONES.

Officers for the Year 1839.

President,
GULIAN C. VERPLANCK.

1st Vice-President,
WASHINGTON IRVING.

2d Vice-President,
PETER SCHERMERHORN.

3d Vice-President,
CORNELIUS HEYER.

4th Vice-President,
EGBERT BENSON.

Treasurer,
JOHN OOTHOUT.

Secretary,
HAMILTON FISH.

Assistant Secretary,
WM. A. LAWRENCE.

Managers,
JAMES R. MANLEY,
THOMAS R. MERCEIN,
ABRAHAM ASTEN,
JOHN LEVERIDGE,
GEORGE B. RAPELYE,
WILLIAM J. VAN WAGENEN,
ROBERT BENSON,
JEROMUS JOHNSON,
JOHN W. MULLIGAN,
ABEL T. ANDERSON,
HENRY BEECKMAN,
JOHN D. CAMPBELL.

Chaplain,
RT. REV. BENJ. T. ONDERDONK.

Physicians,
WILLIAM H. HOBART.
JOHN D. OGDEN.

Consulting Physicians,
JOHN W. FRANCIS,
HUGH M'LEAN.

Stewards,
ALEX. R. WYCKOFF,
DAVID C. COLDEN,
JAMES BOWEN,
ANTHONY J. BLEECKER,
JONATHAN NATHAN,
JOHN A. KING,
JAMES J. JONES.

Officers for the Year 1840.

President,
GULIAN C. VERPLANCK.

1st Vice-President,
WASHINGTON IRVING.

2d Vice-President,
PETER SCHERMERHORN.

3d Vice-President,
CORNELIUS HEYER.

4th Vice-President,
EGBERT BENSON.

Treasurer,
JOHN OOTHOUT.

Secretary,
HAMILTON FISH.

Assistant Secretary,
WM. A. LAWRENCE.

Managers,
JAMES R. MANLEY,
THOMAS R. MERCEIN,
ABRAHAM ASTEN,
GEORGE B. RAPELYE,
WILLIAM J. VAN WAGENEN,
JOHN B. SCHMELZEL,
ROBERT BENSON,
JEROMUS JOHNSON,
JOHN LEVERIDGE,
HENRY BEECKMAN,
SAMUEL G. RAYMOND,
ALEX. I. COTHEAL.

Chaplain,
RT. REV. BENJ. T. ONDERDONK.

Physicians,
WILLIAM H. HOBART,
JOHN D. OGDEN.

Consulting Physicians,
JOHN W. FRANCIS,
HUGH M'LEAN.

Stewards,
ALEX. R. WYCKOFF,
DAVID C. COLDEN,
JAMES BOWEN,
ANTHONY J. BLEECKER,
JONATHAN NATHAN,
JOHN A. KING,
JAMES J. JONES.

Officers for the Year 1841.

President,
GULIAN C. VERPLANCK.

1st Vice President,
WASHINGTON IRVING.

2d Vice-President,
PETER SCHERMERHORN.

3d Vice-President,
CORNELIUS HEYER

4th Vice-President,
EGBERT BENSON.

Treasurer,
JOHN OOTHOUT.

Secretary,
HAMILTON FISH.

Assistant Secretary,
WM. A. LAWRENCE.

Managers,
JAMES R. MANLEY,
THOMAS R. MERCEIN,
JOHN LEVERIDGE,
WILLIAM J. VAN WAGENEN,
JOHN B. SCHMELZEL,
JOHN TURNER,
ROBERT BENSON,
ABRAHAM ASTEN,
GEORGE B. RAPELYE,
SAMUEL G. RAYMOND,
ALEX. I. COTHEAL,
JAMES H. KIP.

Chaplain,
RT. REV. BENJ. T. ONDERDONK.

Physicians,
WILLIAM H. HOBART,
JOHN D. OGDEN,

Consulting Physicians,
JOHN W. FRANCIS,
HUGH M'LEAN.

Stewards,
ALEX. R. WYCKOFF,
DAVID C. COLDEN,
JAMES BOWEN,
ANTHONY J. BLEECKER,
JONATHAN NATHAN,
JOHN A. KING,
JAMES J. JONES.

Officers for the Year 1842.

President,
EGBERT BENSON,

1st Vice-President,
PETER SCHERMERHORN..

2d Vice-President,
WILLIAM J. VAN WAGENEN.

3d Vice-President,
JOHN TURNER.

4th Vice-President,
JAMES R. MANLEY.

Treasurer,
JOHN OOTHOUT.

Secretary,
HAMILTON FISH.

Assistant Secretary,
JAMES MANLEY.

Managers.
ROBERT BENSON,
JOHN LEVERIDGE,
JOHN B. SCHMELZEL,
JAMES H. KIP,
DAVID C. COLDEN,
GEORGE B. RAPELYE,
ABRAHAM ASTEN,
SAMUEL G. RAYMOND,
ALEX. I. COTHEAL,
ABRAHAM R. LAWRENCE,
FREDERIC DE PEYSTER,
JONATHAN NATHAN.

Chaplains,
RT REV. BENJ. T. ONDERDONK,
REV. THOMAS E. VERMILYE.

Physicians,
WM. H. HOBART,
JOHN G. ADAMS.

Consulting Physicians,
JOHN W. FRANCIS,
HUGH M'LEAN.

Stewards,
ALEX. R. WYCKOFF,
JAMES J. JONES,
JACOB R. NEVIUS,
ANTHONY J. BLEECKER,
WILLIAM TURNER,
WILLIAM DUMONT,
M. CHARLES PATERSON.

Officers for the Year 1843.

President,
EGBERT BENSON.

1st Vice-President,
PETER SCHERMERHORN.

2d Vice-President,
WILLIAM J. VAN WAGENEN.

3d Vice-President,
JAMES R. MANLEY.

4th Vice-President,
ABRAHAM R. LAWRENCE.

Treasurer,
JOHN OOTHOUT.

Secretary,
HAMILTON FISH.

Assistant Secretary,
JAMES MANLEY.

Managers,
ROBERT BENSON,
ALEX. I. COTHEAL,
ABRAHAM ASTEN,
SAMUEL G. RAYMOND,
JAMES H. KIP,
DAVID C. COLDEN,
FREDERIC DE PEYSTER,
JOHN LEVERIDGE,
JOHN B. SCHMELZEL,
JONATHAN NATHAN,
WILLIAM H. JOHNSON,
ROBERT KERMIT.

Chaplains,
RT. REV. BENJ. T. ONDERDONK,
REV. THOMAS E. VERMILYE.

Physicians,
WILLIAM H. HOBART,
JACOB HARSEN.

Consulting Physicians,
JOHN W. FRANCIS,
HUGH M'LEAN.

Stewards,
ANTHONY J. BLEECKER,
WILLIAM TURNER,
JACOB R. NEVIUS,
WILLIAM DUMONT,
M. CHARLES PATERSON,
ALEX. R. WYCKOFF,
JOHN D. VAN BEUREN.

Officers for the Year 1844.

President,
JAMES R. MANLEY.

1st Vice-President,
PETER SCHERMERHORN.

2d Vice-President,
WILLIAM J. VAN WAGENEN.

3d Vice-President,
ABRAHAM R. LAWRENCE.

4th Vice-President,
OGDEN HOFFMAN.

Treasurer,
FREDERIC DE PEYSTER.

Secretary,
SAMUEL G. RAYMOND.

Assistant Secretary,
JAMES MANLEY.

Managers,
JOHN LEVERIDGE,
JOHN B. SCHMELZEL,
JAMES H. KIP,
ALEX. I. COTHEAL,
JONATHAN NATHAN,
ROBERT KERMIT,
WILLIAM H. JOHNSON,
JAMES F. DE PEYSTER,
HAMILTON FISH,
SAMUEL JONES,
ANTHONY J. BLEECKER,
THOMAS C. CHARDAVOYNE,

Chaplains,
RT. REV. BENJ. T. ONDERDONK,
REV. THOMAS F. VERMILYE.

Physicians,
WILLIAM H. HOBART,
JACOB HARSEN.

Consulting Physicians,
JOHN W. FRANCIS,
HUGH M'LEAN.

Stewards,
JOHN D. VAN BEUREN,
JACOB R. NEVIUS,
CORNELIUS V. S. ROOSEVELT,
CHARLES F. HOFFMAN,
PETER A. SCHERMERHORN,
DENNING DUER,
JAMES DE PEYSTER OGDEN.

Officers for the Year 1845.

President,
JAMES R. MANLEY.

1st Vice-President,
ABRAHAM R. LAWRENCE.

2d Vice-President,
OGDEN HOFFMAN.

3d Vice-President,
SAMUEL JONES.

4th Vice-President,
JAMES DE PEYSTER OGDEN.

Treasurer,
FREDERIC DE PEYSTER.

Secretary,
SAMUEL G. RAYMOND.

Assistant Secretary,
JAMES MANLEY.

Managers,
JOHN LEVERIDGE,
JAMES H. KIP,
ALEX. I. COTHEAL,
JONATHAN NATHAN,
ROBERT KERMIT,
FRANCIS V. MANY,
JAMES F. DE PEYSTER,
HAMILTON FISH,
DAVID C. COLDEN,
ANTHONY J. BLEECKER,
THOMAS C. CHARDAVOYNE,
HARMAN C. WESTERVELT.

Chaplains,
RT. REV. BENJ. T. ONDERDONK,
REV. THOMAS E. VERMILYE.

Physicians,
WILLIAM H. HOBART,
JACOB HARSEN.

Consulting Physicians,
JOHN W. FRANCIS,
HUGH M'LEAN.

Stewards,
JOHN D. VAN BEUREN,
JACOB R. NEVIUS,
CHARLES F. HOFFMAN,
DENNING DUER,
ALEX. R. WYCKOFF,
WILLIAM TURNER,
DAYTON HOBART.

4

Officers for the Year 1846.

President,
SAMUEL JONES.

1st Vice-President,
ABRAHAM R. LAWRENCE.

2d Vice-President,
OGDEN HOFFMAN.

3d Vice-President,
J. DE PEYSTER OGDEN.

4th Vice-President,
JOHN A. KING.

Treasurer,
WILLIAM H. JOHNSON.

Secretary.
SAMUEL G. RAYMOND

Assistant Secretary,
JAMES MANLEY.

Managers,
JAMES H. KIP,
ALEX. I. COTHEAL,
ROBERT KERMIT,
DAVID C. COLDEN,
WM. J. VAN WAGENEN,
THOMAS C. CHARDAVOYNE,
HAMILTON FISH,
JAMES F. DE PEYSTER,
WILLIAM M. VERMILYE,
HARMAN C. WESTERVELT,
FRANCIS V. MANY,
ABRAHAM FARDON, JR.

Chaplains.
REV. THOMAS E. VERMILYE,
REV. WILLIAM BERRIAN.

Physicians,
WILLIAM H. HOBART,
WILLIAM TURNER.

Consulting Physicians,
JOHN W. FRANCIS,
HUGH M'LEAN.

Stewards,
CHARLES F. HOFFMAN,
PIERRE M. IRVING,
DENNING DUER,
ALEX. R. WYCKOFF,
ISAAC S. HONE,
JAMES BREATH,
LEWIS GAYLORD CLARK.

Officers for the Year 1847.

President,
SAMUEL JONES.

1st Vice-President,
ABRAHAM R. LAWRENCE.

2d Vice-President,
J. DE PEYSTER OGDEN.

3d Vice-President,
JOHN A. KING.

4th Vice-President,
HAMILTON FISH.

Treasurer,
WILLIAM H. JOHNSON.

Secretary,
SAMUEL G. RAYMOND.

Assistant Secretary,
ALEX. I. COTHEAL.

Managers,
JAMES H. KIP,
THOMAS C. CHARDAVOYNE,
WILLIAM M. VERMILYE,
JACOB ANTHONY,
WM. J. VAN WAGENEN,
FRANCIS V. MANY,
ABRAHAM FARDON, JR.,
ELIAS G. DRAKE,
JAMES R. MANLEY,
T. C. WINTHROP,
HARMAN C. WESTERVELT,
JACOB HARSEN.

Chaplains,
REV. THOMAS E. VERMILYE,
REV. WILLIAM BERRIAN.

Physicians,
WILLIAM H. HOBART,
JOHN G. ADAMS.

Consulting Physicians,
JOHN W. FRANCIS,
JOHN C. CHEESMAN.

Stewards,
PIERRE M. IRVING,
LEWIS GAYLORD CLARK,
NICHOLAS LOW,
JAMES BREATH,
CHARLES R. SWORDS,
AARON B. HAYS,
JOHN T. STAGG.

Officers for the Year 1848.

President,
JOHN A. KING.

1st Vice-President,
J. DE PEYSTER OGDEN.

2d Vice-President,
HAMILTON FISH.

3d Vice-President,
OGDEN HOFFMAN.

4th Vice-President,
EGBERT BENSON.

Treasurer,
WILLIAM H. JOHNSON.

Secretary,
SAMUEL G. RAYMOND.

Assistant Secretary,
ALEX. I. COTHEAL.

Managers,
JAMES H. KIP,
THOMAS C. CHARDAVOYNE,
WILLIAM M. VERMILYE,
JACOB ANTHONY,
WM. J. VAN WAGENEN,
FRANCIS V. MANY,
ABRAHAM FARDON, JR.,
ELIAS G. DRAKE,
JAMES R. MANLEY,
HARMAN C. WESTERVELT,
CHARLES R. SWORDS,
JACOB R. NEVIUS.

Chaplains,
REV. THOMAS E. VERMILYE,
REV. WILLIAM L. JOHNSON.

Physicians,
WILLIAM H. HOBART,
JOHN G. ADAMS.

Consulting Physicians,
JOHN W. FRANCIS,
JOHN C. CHEESMAN.

Stewards,
CHARLES R. SWORDS,
JAMES BREATH,
NICHOLAS LOW,
PIERRE M. IRVING,
LEWIS GAYLORD CLARK,
AARON B. HAYS,
JOHN T. STAGG.

Officers for the Year 1849.

President,
JOHN A. KING.

1st Vice-President,
J. DE PEYSTER OGDEN.

2d Vice-President,
HAMILTON FISH.

3d Vice President,
OGDEN HOFFMAN.

4th Vice-President,
JAMES H. KIP.

Treasurer,
WILLIAM H. JOHNSON.

Secretary,
ALEX. I. COTHEAL.

Assistant Secretary.
CHARLES R. SWORDS.

Managers,
SAMUEL JONES,
EGBERT BENSON,
SAMUEL G. RAYMOND,
THOMAS C. CHARDAVOYNE,
JACOB ANTHONY,
WILLIAM J. VAN WAGENEN,
ABRAHAM FARDON, JR.,
ELIAS G. DRAKE,
JAMES R. MANLEY,
PIERRE M. IRVING,
AARON B. HAYS,
JOHN J. CISCO.

Chaplains.
REV. THOMAS E. VERMILYE,
REV. WILLIAM L. JOHNSON.

Physicians.
WILLIAM H. HOBART,
JOHN G. ADAMS.

Consulting Physicians,
JOHN W. FRANCIS,
JOHN C. CHEESMAN.

Stewards,
JAMES BREATH,
NICHOLAS LOW,
DAYTON HOBART,
DENNING DUER,
ALEXANDER E. HOSACK,
GERARD STUYVESANT,
RICHARD H. OGDEN.

Officers for the Year 1850.

President,
JAMES DE PEYSTER OGDEN.

1st Vice-President,
HAMILTON FISH.

2d Vice-President,
OGDEN HOFFMAN.

3d Vice-President,
JAMES H. KIP.

4th Vice-President,
SAMUEL G. RAYMOND.

Treasurer,
WILLIAM H. JOHNSON.

Secretary,
ALEX. I. COTHEAL.

Assistant-Secretary,
CHARLES R. SWORDS.

Managers,
SAMUEL JONES,
JACOB ANTHONY,
WILLIAM J. VAN WAGENEN,
ABRAHAM FARDON, JR.,
JAMES R. MANLEY,
PIERRE M. IRVING,
AARON B. HAYS,
FREDERIC DE PEYSTER,
JOHN J. CISCO,
JOHN W. LIVINGSTON,
JAMES J. ROOSEVELT,
JAMES BREATH.

Chaplains.
REV. THOMAS E. VERMILYE,
REV. WILLIAM L. JOHNSON.

Physicians,
WILLIAM H. HOBART,
JOHN G. ADAMS.

Consulting Physicians,
JOHN W. FRANCIS,
JOHN C. CHEESMAN.

Stewards,
NICHOLAS LOW,
RICHARD H. OGDEN,
HENRY A. HEISER,
JOHN ROMEYN BRODHEAD,
JAMES WATSON WEBB,
JAMES W. BEEKMAN,
ELIAS G. DRAKE.

Officers for the Year
1851.

President,
JAMES DE PEYSTER OGDEN.

1st Vice-President,
HAMILTON FISH.

2d Vice President,
OGDEN HOFFMAN.

3d Vice-President,
JAMES H. KIP.

4th Vice-President,
JOHN W. FRANCIS.

Treasurer.
WILLIAM H. JOHNSON.

Secretary,
CHARLES R. SWORDS.

Assistant Secretary,
RICHARD E. MOUNT, JR.

Managers,
SAMUEL JONES,
JAMES R. MANLEY,
WILLIAM J. VAN WAGENEN,
JACOB ANTHONY,
JOHN W. LIVINGSTON,
FREDERIC DE PEYSTER,
AARON B. HAYS,
JAMES J. ROOSEVELT,
CHARLES KING,
CORNELIUS OAKLEY,
SYLVESTER L. H. WARD,
AMBROSE C. KINGSLAND.

Chaplains.
REV. THOMAS E. VERMILYE,
REV. WILLIAM L. JOHNSON.

Physicians,
WILLIAM H. HOBART,
JOHN G. ADAMS.

Consulting Physicians.
JOHN C. CHEESMAN,
J. KEARNY RODGERS.

Stewards,
JAMES W. BEEKMAN,
J. ROMEYN BRODHEAD,
ELIAS G. DRAKE,
NICHOLAS LOW,
HENRY A. HEISER,
JAMES BREATH,
JOHN J. CISCO.

Officers for the Year
1852.

President,,
OGDEN HOFFMAN.

1st Vice-President,
HAMILTON FISH.

2d Vice-President,
JAMES H. KIP.

3d Vice-President,
JOHN W. FRANCIS.

4th Vice-President,
FREDERIC DE PEYSTER.

Treasurer,
WILLIAM H. JOHNSON.

Secretary,
CHARLES R. SWORDS.

Assistant Secretary,
RICHARD E. MOUNT, JR.

Managers,
SAMUEL JONES,
JOHN W. LIVINGSTON,
WILLIAM J. VAN WAGENEN,
JACOB ANTHONY,
JAMES J. ROOSEVELT,
CORNELIUS OAKLEY,
SYLVESTER L. H. WARD,
AMBROSE C. KINGSLAND,
JAMES W. BEEKMAN,
BENJAMIN H. FIELD,
JOHN G. ADAMS,
D. HENRY HAIGHT.

Chaplains.
REV. THOMAS E. VERMILYE,
REV. WILLIAM L. JOHNSON.

Physicians,
BENJAMIN DRAKE,
WILLIAM H. JACKSON.

Consulting Physicians,
JOHN C. CHEESMAN,
JAMES R. MANLEY.

Stewards,
NICHOLAS LOW,
J. ROMEYN BRODHEAD,
PIERRE M. IRVING,
JOHN J. CISCO,
AARON B. HAYS,
AUGUSTUS SCHELL,
WILLIAM J. BUNKER.

Officers for the Year 1853.

President,
OGDEN HOFFMAN.

1st Vice-President,
HAMILTON FISH.

2d Vice-President,
JAMES H. KIP.

3d Vice-President,
JOHN W. FRANCIS.

4th Vice-President,
FREDERIC DE PEYSTER.

Treasurer.
WILLIAM H. JOHNSON.

Secretary,
CHARLES R. SWORDS.

Assistant Secretary,
RICHARD E. MOUNT, JR.

Managers,
SAMUEL JONES,
WM. J. VAN WAGENEN,
JACOB ANTHONY,
CORNELIUS OAKLEY,
JAMES J. ROOSEVELT,
JAMES W. BEEKMAN,
SYLVESTER L. H. WARD,
JOHN G. ADAMS,
D. HENRY HAIGHT,
ALEX. I. COTHEAL,
JOHN D. VAN BUREN,
JOHN RIDLEY.

Chaplains.
REV. THOMAS E. VERMILYE,
REV. WILLIAM L. JOHNSON.

Physicians,
BENJAMIN DRAKE,
WILLIAM H. JACKSON.

Consulting Physicians,
JOHN C. CHEESMAN,
RICHARD S. KISSAM.

Stewards,
NICHOLAS LOW,
J. ROMEYN BRODHEAD,
JOHN J. CISCO,
AUGUSTUS SCHELL,
AARON B. HAYS,
GERRIT G. VAN WAGENEN,
BENJAMIN H. FIELD.

Officers for the Year 1854.

President.
FREDERIC DE PEYSTER.

1st Vice-President,
HAMILTON FISH.

2d Vice-President,
JOHN W. FRANCIS.

3d Vice-President,
JAMES J. ROOSEVELT.

4th Vice-President,
J. ROMEYN BRODHEAD.

Treasurer,
WILLIAM H. JOHNSON.

Secretary,
CHARLES R. SWORDS.

Assistant Secretary,
RICHARD E. MOUNT, JR.

Managers,
WILLIAM J. VAN WAGENEN,
JACOB ANTHONY,
CORNELIUS OAKLEY,
JAMES W. BEEKMAN,
SYLVESTER L. H. WARD,
D. HENRY HAIGHT,
ALEX. I. COTHEAL,
JOHN RIDLEY,
ELIAS G. DRAKE,
NICHOLAS LOW,
JOHN J. CISCO,
JAMES H. KIP.

Chaplains,
REV. THOMAS E. VERMILYE,
REV. WILLIAM L. JOHNSON.

Physicians,
BENJAMIN DRAKE,
ABRAM DUBOIS.

Consulting Physicians,
JOHN C. CHEESMAN,
RICHARD S. KISSAM.

Stewards,
GERRIT G. VAN WAGENEN,
BENJAMIN H. FIELD,
JOHN VAN BUREN,
WILLIAM DUMONT,
ADRIAN B. HOLMES,
PETER H. VANDERVOORT,
EDWARD SLOSSON.

Officers for the Year 1855.

President,
FREDERIC DE PEYSTER.
1st Vice-President,
HAMILTON FISH.
2d Vice-President,
JAMES J. ROOSEVELT.
3d Vice-President,
JOHN ROMEYN BRODHEAD.
4th Vice-President,
GERRIT G. VAN WAGENEN.
Treasurer,
WILLIAM H. JOHNSON.
Secretary,
CHARLES R. SWORDS.
Assistant Secretary,
RICHARD E. MOUNT, JR.
Managers,
WILLIAM J. VAN WAGENEN,
JACOB ANTHONY,
CORNELIUS OAKLEY,
SYLVESTER L. H. WARD,
ELIAS G. DRAKE,
JOHN J. CISCO,
JAMES H. KIP,
JAMES DE PEYSTER OGDEN,
AUGUSTUS SCHELL,
WILLIAM DUMONT,
JAMES MANLEY,
JOHN ALSTYNE.
Chaplains,
REV. THOMAS E. VERMILYE,
REV. WILLIAM L. JOHNSON.
Physicians,
RICHARD S. KISSAM,
EDWARD L. BEADLE.
Consulting Physicians,
JOHN W. FRANCIS,
JOHN C. CHEESMAN.
Stewards,
JOHN VAN BUREN,
PETER H. VANDERVOORT,
ADRIAN B. HOLMES,
BENJAMIN H. FIELD,
D. HENRY HAIGHT,
ALEX. J. COTHEAL,
DUNCAN F. CURRY.

Officers for the Year 1856.

President,
JAMES DE PEYSTER OGDEN.
1st Vice-President,
HAMILTON FISH.
2d Vice-President,
JAMES J. ROOSEVELT.
3d Vice-President,
JOHN R. BRODHEAD.
4th Vice-President,
GERRIT G. VAN WAGENEN.
Treasurer,
WILLIAM H. JOHNSON.
Secretary,
CHARLES R. SWORDS.
Assistant Secretary,
RICHARD E. MOUNT, JR.
Managers,
WILLIAM J. VAN WAGENEN,
JACOB ANTHONY,
CORNELIUS OAKLEY,
SYLVESTER L. H. WARD,
FREDERIC DE PEYSTER,
JOHN J. CISCO,
JAMES H. KIP,
BENJAMIN H. FIELD,
AUGUSTUS SCHELL,
WILLIAM DUMONT,
JAMES MANLEY,
JOHN ALSTYNE.
Chaplains,
REV. THOMAS E. VERMILYE,
REV. WILLIAM L. JOHNSON.
Physicians,
RICHARD S. KISSAM,
EDWARD L. BEADLE.
Consulting Physicians,
JOHN W. FRANCIS,
JOHN C. CHEESMAN.
Stewards,
JOHN VAN BUREN,
ADRIAN B. HOLMES,
D. HENRY HAIGHT,
ALEXANDER I. COTHEAL,
DUNCAN F. CURRY,
PETER H. VANDERVOORT,
JAMES BREATH.

Officers for the Year 1857.

President,
JAMES DE PEYSTER OGDEN.

1st Vice-President,
HAMILTON FISH.

2d Vice-President,
JAMES J. ROOSEVELT.

3d Vice-President,
JOHN R. BRODHEAD.

4th Vice-President,
GERRIT G. VAN WAGENEN.

Treasurer,
WILLIAM H. JOHNSON.

Secretary,
CHARLES R. SWORDS.

Assistant Secretary,
RICHARD E. MOUNT, JR.

Managers,
WILLIAM J. VAN WAGENEN,
CORNELIUS OAKLEY,
SYLVESTER L. H. WARD,
FREDERIC DE PEYSTER,
JOHN J. CISCO,
JAMES H. KIP,
BENJAMIN H. FIELD,
AUGUSTUS SCHELL,
WILLIAM DUMONT,
JAMES MANLEY,
JOHN ALSTYNE,
JAMES W. BEEKMAN.

Chaplains,
REV. THOMAS E VERMILYE,
REV. WILLIAM L. JOHNSON.

Physicians,
RICHARD S. KISSAM,
EDWARD L. BEADLE.

Consulting Physicians,
JOHN W. FRANCIS,
JOHN C. CHEESMAN.

Stewards,
JOHN VAN BUREN,
PETER H. VANDERVOORT,
JAMES BREATH,
DUNCAN F. CURRY,
BENJAMIN R. WINTHROP,
ALEXANDER J. COTHEAL,
HARMAN C. WESTERVELT.

Officers for the Year 1858.

President,
GULIAN C. VERPLANCK.

1st Vice-President,
HAMILTON FISH.

2d Vice-President,
JAMES J. ROOSEVELT.

3d Vice-President,
JOHN R. BRODHEAD.

4th Vice-President,
GERRIT G. VAN WAGENEN.

Treasurer,
WILLIAM H. JOHNSON.

Secretary,
JOHN G. ADAMS.

Assistant Secretary,
WORTHINGTON ROMAINE.

Managers,
WILLIAM J. VAN WAGENEN,
FREDERIC DE PEYSTER,
JOHN J. CISCO,
BENJAMIN H. FIELD,
AUGUSTUS SCHELL,
JAMES H. KIP,
JOHN ALSTYNE,
JAMES W. BEEKMAN,
JAMES MANLEY,
JAMES DE P. OGDEN,
WILLIAM DUMONT,
ANDREW WARNER.

Chaplains,
REV. THOMAS E. VERMILYE,
REV. WILLIAM L. JOHNSON.

Physicians,
EDWARD L. BEADLE,
JAMES ANDERSON.

Consulting Physicians,
JOHN W. FRANCIS,
JOHN C. CHEESMAN.

Stewards,
JOHN VAN BUREN,
PETER H. VANDERVOORT,
JOHN D. VAN BUREN,
CHARLES VANDERVOORT,
GERRIT G. VAN WAGENEN,
EDGAR S. VAN WINKLE,
WILLIAM J. VAN WAGENEN.

Officers for the Year 1859.

President,
GULIAN C. VERPLANCK.

1st Vice-President,
JAMES J. ROOSEVELT.

2d Vice-President,
JOHN R. BRODHEAD.

3d Vice President,
JACOB HARSEN.

4th Vice-President,
CHARLES R. SWORDS.

Treasurer,
WILLIAM M. VERMILYE.

Secretary.
RICHARD E. MOUNT, JR.

Assistant Secretary,
WORTHINGTON ROMAINE

Managers,
WILLIAM J. VAN WAGENEN,
FREDERIC DE PEYSTER,
JOHN J. CISCO,
BENJAMIN H. FIELD,
AUGUSTUS SCHELL,
JAMES H. KIP,
JOHN ALSTYNE,
JAMES W. BEEKMAN,
JAMES MANLEY,
JAMES DE P. OGDEN,
WILLIAM DUMONT,
ANDREW WARNER.

Chaplains,
REV. THOMAS E. VERMILYE,
REV. WILLIAM L. JOHNSON.

Physicians,
EDWARD L. BEADLE,
ABRAM DUBOIS.

Consulting Physicians,
JOHN W. FRANCIS,
JOHN C. CHEESMAN.

Stewards,
JOHN VAN BUREN,
JAMES H. PINKNEY,
AARON B. HAYS,
JOHN D. VAN BUREN,
CHARLES ROOME,
WILLIAM H. JOHNSON,
JOHN GROSHON.

Officers for the Year 1860.

President.
HAMILTON FISH.

1st Vice-President,
JAMES J. ROOSEVELT.

2d Vice-President,
JOHN R. BRODHEAD.

3d Vice-President,
JACOB HARSEN.

4th Vice-President,
CHARLES R. SWORDS.

Treasurer,
WILLIAM M. VERMILYE.

Secretary,
RICHARD E. MOUNT, JR.

Assistant Secretary,
WORTHINGTON ROMAINE.

Managers,
GULIAN C. VERPLANCK,
JAMES DE P. OGDEN,
FREDERIC DE PEYSTER,
JOHN J. CISCO,
BENJAMIN H. FIELD,
AUGUSTUS SCHELL,
JAMES H. KIP,
JOHN ALSTYNE,
JAMES W. BEEKMAN,
WILLIAM DUMONT,
JAMES MANLEY,
WILLIAM H. JOHNSON.

Chaplains.
REV. THOMAS E. VERMILYE,
REV. WILLIAM L. JOHNSON.

Physicians,
JAMES ANDERSON,
EDWARD L. BEADLE.

Consulting Physicians,
JOHN W. FRANCIS,
JOHN C. CHEESMAN.

Stewards,
JAMES H. PINKNEY,
CHARLES ROOME,
JAMES BREATH,
WASHINGTON R. VERMILYE,
RICHARD L. SUYDAM,
JOHN G. STORM,
JOHN GROSHON.

Officers for the Year 1861.

President,
HAMILTON FISH.

1st Vice-President,
JAMES J. ROOSEVELT.

2d Vice-President.
JOHN VAN BUREN.

3d Vice President,
JOHN R. BRODHEAD.

4th Vice-President,
CHARLES R. SWORDS.

Treasurer,
WILLIAM M. VERMILYE.

Secretary,
RICHARD E. MOUNT, JR.

Assistant Secretary.
WORTHINGTON ROMAINE.

Managers,
GULIAN C. VERPLANCK,
JAMES DE P. OGDEN,
FREDERIC DE PEYSTER,
JOHN J. CISCO,
BENJAMIN H. FIELD,
AUGUSTUS SCHELL,
JOHN ALSTYNE,
JAMES W. BEEKMAN,
WILLIAM DUMONT,
JAMES MANLEY,
WILLIAM H. JOHNSON,
JACOB HARSEN.

Chaplains.
REV. THOMAS E. VERMILYE,
REV. WILLIAM L. JOHNSON.

Physicians.
EDWARD L. BEADLE,
JAMES R. WOOD.

Consulting Physicians,
JOHN W. FRANCIS,
JAMES ANDERSON.

Stewards.
CHARLES ROOME,
JAMES H. PINKNEY,
JOHN D. VAN BUREN,
JAMES BREATH,
EDWARD SCHELL,
JAMES M. McLEAN,
EDWARD SLOSSON.

Officers for the Year 1862.

President,
JAMES J. ROOSEVELT.

1st Vice-President,
JACOB HARSEN.

2d Vice-President,
JOHN VAN BUREN.

3d Vice President,
AUGUSTUS SCHELL.

4th Vice-President,
CHARLES ROOME.

Treasurer,
WILLIAM M. VERMILYE.

Secretary.
RICHARD E. MOUNT, JR.

Assistant Secretary,
WORTHINGTON ROMAINE.

Managers,
GULIAN C. VERPLANCK,
JAMES DE P. OGDEN,
JOHN J. CISCO,
WILLIAM H. JOHNSON,
CHARLES R. SWORDS,
BENJAMIN H. FIELD,
HAMILTON FISH,
FREDERIC DE PEYSTER,
JAMES W. BEEKMAN,
JOHN R. BRODHEAD,
JOHN ALSTYNE,
WILLIAM DUMONT.

Chaplains.
REV. THOMAS E. VERMILYE,
REV. WILLIAM L. JOHNSON.

Physicians,
WILLIAM ROCKWELL,
WILLIAM E. VERMILYE.

Consulting Physicians,
JAMES ANDERSON,
JAMES R. WOOD.

Stewards,
JAMES H. PINKNEY,
EDWARD SLOSSON,
CLAUDIUS L. MONELL,
JAMES M. McLEAN,
EDWARD SCHELL,
CARLISLE NORWOOD,
AUGUSTUS R. MACDONOUGH.

Officers for the Year 1863.

President.
JOHN VAN BUREN.

1st Vice-President,
AUGUSTUS SCHELL.

2d Vice-President,
CHARLES ROOME.

3d Vice-President,
JAMES W. BEEKMAN.

4th Vice-President.
BENJAMIN H. FIELD.

Treasurer,
WILLIAM M. VERMILYE.

Secretary,
RICHARD E. MOUNT, JR.

Assistant Secretary,
WORTHINGTON ROMAINE.

Managers,
GULIAN C. VERPLANCK,
JOHN J. CISCO,
WILLIAM H. JOHNSON,
JAMES J. ROOSEVELT,
HAMILTON FISH,
JOHN ALSTYNE,
JAMES DE P. OGDEN,
FREDERIC DE PEYSTER,
CHARLES R. SWORDS,
JACOB HARSEN,
D. HENRY HAIGHT,
WILLIAM DUMONT.

Chaplains,
REV. THOMAS E. VERMILYE,
REV. WILLIAM L. JOHNSON.

Physicians,
WILLIAM ROCKWELL,
WILLIAM E. VERMILYE,

Consulting Physicians,
JAMES ANDERSON,
JAMES R. WOOD.

Stewards.
EDWARD H. ARTHUR,
AUGUSTUS R. MACDONOUGH,
ROBERT G. REMSEN,
DAYTON HOBART,
GEORGE W. MCLEAN,
JAMES A. SUYDAM,
WILLIAM IRVING GRAHAM.

Officers for the Year 1864.

President,
JAMES J. ROOSEVELT.

1st Vice-President,
AUGUSTUS SCHELL.

2d Vice-President,
CHARLES ROOME,

3d Vice-President,
JAMES W. BEEKMAN.

4th Vice-President,
BENJAMIN H. FIELD,

Treasurer,
WILLIAM M. VERMILYE,

Secretary,
RICHARD E. MOUNT, JR.

Assistant Secretary.
WORTHINGTON ROMAINE.

Managers,
GULIAN C. VERPLANCK,
HAMILTON FISH,
JOHN VAN BUREN,
WILLIAM H. JOHNSON,
CHARLES R. SWORDS,
WILLIAM DUMONT,
JAMES DE PEYSTER OGDEN,
FREDERIC DE PEYSTER,
JOHN J. CISCO,
JOHN ALSTYNE,
D. HENRY HAIGHT,
JAMES M. MCLEAN.

Chaplains,
REV. THOMAS E. VERMILYE,
REV. WILLIAM L. JOHNSON.

Physicians,
WILLIAM ROCKWELL,
WILLIAM E. VERMILYE.

Consulting Physicians,
JAMES ANDERSON,
JAMES R. WOOD.

Stewards,
EDWARD H. ARTHUR,
ROBERT G. REMSEN,
EDWARD SLOSSON,
AUGUSTUS R. MACDONOUGH,
WILLIAM IRVING GRAHAM,
JAMES A. SUYDAM,
GEORGE W. MCLEAN.

Officers for the Year
1865.

President,
AUGUSTUS SCHELL.
1st Vice President,
CHARLES ROOME.
2d Vice-President,
JAMES W. BEEKMAN.
3d Vice-President,
BENJAMIN H. FIELD.
4th Vice-President,
RICHARD E. MOUNT, JR.
Treasurer,
WILLIAM M. VERMILYE.
Secretary,
AUGUSTUS R. MACDONOUGH.
Assistant Secretary,
ARCHIBALD S. VAN DUZER.
Managers,
GULIAN C. VERPLANCK,
JAMES DE P. OGDEN,
JOHN VAN BUREN,
WILLIAM H. JOHNSON,
CHARLES R. SWORDS,
WILLIAM DUMONT,
HAMILTON FISH,
FREDERIC DE PEYSTER,
JAMES J. ROOSEVELT,
JOHN ALSTYNE,
D. HENRY HAIGHT,
JAMES M. McLEAN.
Chaplains.
REV. THOMAS E. VERMILYE,
REV. WILLIAM L. JOHNSON.
Physicians,
ABRAM DUBOIS,
WILLIAM E. VERMILYE.
Consulting Physicians,
JAMES ANDERSON,
JAMES R. WOOD.
Stewards,
EDWARD H. ARTHUR,
WILLIAM IRVING GRAHAM,
GEORGE W. McLEAN,
ROBERT G. REMSEN,
JAMES A. SUYDAM,
JAMES BREATH,
EDWARD SLOSSON.

Officers for the Year
1866.

President,
AUGUSTUS SCHELL,
1st Vice-President,
CHARLES ROOME.
2d Vice President,
JAMES W. BEEKMAN,
3d Vice-President,
BENJAMIN H. FIELD.
4th Vice-President,
RICHARD E. MOUNT, JR.
Treasurer,
WILLIAM M. VERMILYE,
Secretary,
AUGUSTUS R. MACDONOUGH.
Assistant Secretary,
ARCHIBALD S. VAN DUZER.
Managers,
GULIAN C. VERPLANCK,
JAMES DE P. OGDEN,
JOHN VAN BUREN,
WILLIAM H. JOHNSON,
CHARLES R. SWORDS,
JAMES M. McLEAN,
HAMILTON FISH,
FREDERIC DE PEYSTER,
JAMES J. ROOSEVELT,
JOHN ALSTYNE,
D. HENRY HAIGHT,
AARON B. HAYS.
Chaplains.
REV. THOMAS E. VERMILYE,
REV. WILLIAM L. JOHNSON.
Physicians,
ABRAM DUBOIS,
WILLIAM E. VERMILYE.
Consulting Physicians,
JAMES ANDERSON,
JAMES R. WOOD.
Stewards.
EDWARD H. ARTHUR,
ROBERT G. REMSEN,
JAMES BREATH,
WM. IRVING GRAHAM,
GEORGE W. McLEAN,
EDWARD SLOSSON,
CHARLES VANDERVOORT.

Officers for the Year 1867.

President,
CHARLES ROOME.

1st Vice-President,
JAMES W. BEEKMAN.

2d Vice-President,
BENJAMIN H. FIELD.

3d Vice President,
RICHARD E. MOUNT, JR.

4th Vice President,
JAMES M. McLEAN.

Treasurer,
WILLIAM M. VERMILYE.

Secretary,
AUGUSTUS R. MACDONOUGH.

Assistant Secretary,
ARCHIBALD S. VAN DUZER.

Managers,
GULIAN C. VERPLANCK,
WILLIAM H. JOHNSON,
CHARLES R. SWORDS,
D. HENRY HAIGHT,
JOHN ALSTYNE,
AARON B. HAYS,
JAMES DE P. OGDEN,
FREDERIC DE PEYSTER,
JAMES J. ROOSEVELT,
AUGUSTUS SCHELL,
HAMILTON FISH,
WILLIAM REMSEN.

Chaplains,
REV. THOMAS E. VERMILYE,
REV. WILLIAM L. JOHNSON.

Physicians,
ABRAM DUBOIS,
WILLIAM E. VERMILYE.

Consulting Physicians,
JAMES ANDERSON,
JAMES R. WOOD.

Stewards,
EDWARD H. ARTHUR,
GEORGE W. McLEAN,
ROBERT G. REMSEN,
WILLIAM IRVING GRAHAM,
JAMES BREATH,
EDWARD SLOSSON,
N. W. STUYVESANT CATLIN.

Officers for the Year 1868.

President,
JAMES W. BEEKMAN.

1st Vice-President,
BENJAMIN H. FIELD.

2d Vice-President,
RICHARD E. MOUNT, JR.

3d Vice-President,
JAMES M. McLEAN.

4th Vice-President.
JOHN T. HOFFMAN.

Treasurer,
WILLIAM M. VERMILYE.

Secretary.
AUGUSTUS R. MACDONOUGH.

Assistant Secretary,
SMITH E. LANE.

Managers,
GULIAN C. VERPLANCK,
WILLIAM H. JOHNSON,
CHARLES R. SWORDS,
D. HENRY HAIGHT,
JOHN ALSTYNE,
AARON B. HAYS,
JAMES DE P. OGDEN,
FREDERIC DE PEYSTER,
JAMES J. ROOSEVELT,
AUGUSTUS SCHELL,
CHARLES ROOME,
WILLIAM REMSEN.

Chaplains,
REV. THOMAS E. VERMILYE,
REV. WILLIAM L. JOHNSON.

Physicians,
ABRAM DUBOIS,
WILLIAM E. VERMILYE.

Consulting Physicians,
JAMES ANDERSON,
JAMES R. WOOD.

Stewards,
GEORGE W. McLEAN,
ROBERT G. REMSEN,
ABRAM R. LAWRENCE, JR.,
WILLIAM IRVING GRAHAM,
JAMES BREATH,
CARLISLE NORWOOD,
N. W. STUYVESANT CATLIN.

Officers for the Year 1869.

President,
JAMES W. BEEKMAN.

1st Vice President,
BENJAMIN H. FIELD.

2d Vice-President,
RICHARD E. MOUNT, JR.

3d Vice President,
JAMES M. McLEAN.

4th Vice-President,
JOHN T. HOFFMAN.

Treasurer,
WILLIAM M. VERMILYE.

Secretary,
AUGUSTUS R. MACDONOUGH.

Assistant Secretary,
SMITH E. LANE.

Managers,
GULIAN C. VERPLANCK,
FREDERIC DE PEYSTER,
WILLIAM H. JOHNSON,
CHARLES R. SWORDS,
AUGUSTUS SCHELL,
WILLIAM REMSEN,
JAMES DE P. OGDEN,
JOHN ALSTYNE,
JAMES J. ROOSEVELT,
D. HENRY HAIGHT,
AARON B. HAYS,
CHARLES ROOME.

Chaplains,
REV. THOMAS E. VERMILYE,
REV. WILLIAM L. JOHNSON.

Physicians,
ABRAM DUBOIS,
WILLIAM E. VERMILYE.

Consulting Physicians,
JAMES ANDERSON,
JAMES R. WOOD.

Stewards,
WM. IRVING GRAHAM,
ROBERT G. REMSEN,
CARLISLE NORWOOD,
JAMES BREATH,
N. W. STUYVESANT CATLIN,
SMITH CLIFT,
JOHN FOWLER, JR.

Officers for the Year 1870.

President,
BENJAMIN H. FIELD.

1st Vice-President,
RICHARD E. MOUNT, JR.

2d Vice President,
JAMES M. McLEAN.

3d Vice-President,
JOHN T. HOFFMAN.

4th Vice-President,
AUGUSTUS R. MACDONOUGH.

Treasurer,
WILLIAM M. VERMILYE.

Secretary,
SMITH E. LANE.

Assistant Secretary,
JOHN C. MILLS.

Managers,
GULIAN C. VERPLANCK,
FREDERIC DE PEYSTER,
CHARLES ROOME,
CHARLES R. SWORDS,
WILLIAM H. JOHNSON,
WILLIAM REMSEN,
JAMES DE P. OGDEN,
JAMES J. ROOSEVELT,
AUGUSTUS SCHELL,
AARON B. HAYS,
D. HENRY HAIGHT,
JAMES W. BEEKMAN.

Chaplains,
REV. THOMAS E. VERMILYE,
REV. WILLIAM L. JOHNSON.

Physicians,
ABRAM DUBOIS,
WILLIAM E. VERMILYE,

Consulting Physicians,
JAMES ANDERSON,
JAMES R. WOOD.

Stewards,
WILLIAM IRVING GRAHAM,
N. W. STUYVESANT CATLIN,
SMITH CLIFT,
JAMES BREATH,
CARLISLE NORWOOD,
JOHN FOWLER, JR.,
BENJAMIN L. SWAN.

5

List of Members.

MARCH 4, 1870.

A

ABEEL, GEORGE.
AYMAR, BENJAMIN.
ADAMS, JOHN G.
ANTHONY, NICHOLAS K.
AUSTIN, WILLIAM.
ANTHONY, HENRY T.
ALLEN, WILLIAM M.
ANDERSON, JAMES.
ADRIANCE, JOHN.
ANTHON, GEORGE C.
ACKERT, ALFRED T.
ALVORD, ALWYN A.

B

BOWEN, JAMES.
BREATH, JAMES.
BOGERT, HENRY K.
BELL, GEORGE.
BININGER, ANDREW G.
BETTS, WILLIAM.
BRODHEAD, J. ROMEYN.
BEEKMAN, JAMES W.
BININGER, ABRAHAM.
BOORAEM, AUGUSTUS C.
BAKER, JOHN.
BUSHNELL, CHARLES J.
BEADLE, EDWARD L.

BUCKMASTER, THOS. H.
BOYCE, GERARDUS.
BOWNE, RICHARD H.
BOORAEM, WILLIAM E.
BENEDICT, ERASTUS C.
BOYD, JAMES R.
BREATH, CHARLES.
BEEKMAN, JAMES H.
BEECKMAN, GILBERT L.
BIXBY, FRANCIS M.
BARGER, SAMUEL F.
BENSON, BENJAMIN L.
BAYLEY, WILLIAM A.
BEEKMAN, JAS. W., JR.
BEEKMAN, GERARD.
BALDWIN, THEODORE E.
BOYD, JOHN J., JR.

C

CHARDAVOYNE, THOS. C.
COTHEAL, ALEXANDER I.
COLVILL, ALFRED.
CISCO, JOHN J.
CHEESMAN, TIMOTHY M.
COLVILL, JOHN.
CURRY, DUNCAN F.
CHEESMAN, OSCAR.

CLEMENTS, JAMES W. G.
COCHRANE, JOHN.
CUNNINGHAM, JAMES B.
COOKE, EDWARD G.
CUNNINGHAM, JOHN.
CUNNINGHAM, LEWIS.
COX, WILLIAM A.
COOPER, EDWARD.
CATLIN, N. W. STUYVESANT.
COMBES. R. CARMAN.
CLIFT, SMITH.
COLVILL, JOHN.
CURRIE, CHARLES P.
CASE, ROBERT L.
CORNWELL, DANIEL H.

D

DEPEYSTER, FREDERIC.
DEPEYSTER, JAMES F.
DUMONT, ROBERT.
DASH, JOHN B.
DRAKE, BENJAMIN.
DUBOIS, ABRAM.
DRAKE, JOHN J.
DELAFIELD, EDWARD.
DUMONT, J. LUDLOW.
DEPEYSTER, J. WATTS.
DURYEE, ABRAHAM.
DUMONT, ROBERT S.
DODGE, ROBERT.
DEPEYSTER, J. ASHTON.
DEAN, GILBERT.
DAVIS, SAMUEL C.
DEPEYSTER, EDGAR,
DEPEYSTER, GERARD B.
DUDLEY, HENRY.
DEPEYSTER, FRED'K J.
DOREMUS, R. OGDEN.
DEDERICK, ZACHARIAH.

E

EIGENBRODT, DAVID L.
ERBEN, HENRY.
ERBEN, HENRY, Jr.
ELY, SMITH, Jr.

F

FERRIS, CLAIBORNE.
FIELD, MAUNSELL B.
FISH, HAMILTON.
FIELD, BENJAMIN H.
FIELD, CORTLANDT DE P.
FIELD, WILLIAM H.
FOWLER, FREDERICK R.
FRYER, ISAAC.
FORREST, GEORGE J.
FELLOWS, RICHARD C.
FORBES, PAUL S.
FEARING C. F.
FOWLER, JOHN, Jr.

G

GILBERT, CLINTON.
GRAHAM, WM. IRVING.
GILES, JOHN S.
GERRY, ELDRIDGE T.
GAINES, STEPHEN W.
GOURLIE, JOHN H.
GREENE, JOHN W.

H

HOFFMAN, MURRAY.
HAYS, AARON B.
HEISER, HENRY A.
HAIGHT, D. HENRY.
HAMILTON, ALEX., Jr.
HOOK, GULIAN.
HOLMES, ADRIAN B.
HAYS, DEWITT C.

HAYS, WILLIAM J.
HOOGLAND, ANDREW.
HAMERSLEY, A. GORDON.
HOOK, JOHN DE WINT.
HAMERSLEY, JOHN W.
HOFFMAN, LINDLEY M.
HENRY, PHILIP, JR.
HALSEY, GEORGE A.
HALL, A. OAKEY.
HERRICK, J. HOBART.
HOFFMAN, W. O.
HERRIOT, J. GROSHON.
HAIGHT, EDWARD.
HAND, C. A.
HOFFMAN, JOHN T.
HEGEMAN, WILLIAM.
HALSEY, JACOB L.

I

IRVING, JOHN T.
IRVING, PIERRE M.

J

JOHNSON, WILLIAM H.
JOHNSON, WILLIAM L.
JAY, JOHN.
JONES, JOHN Q.
JACKSON, WILLIAM H.
JONES, GEORGE.
JONES, GEORGE F.
JACOBUS, LYMAN A.

K

KEMBLE, WILLIAM.
KIERSTED, HENRY T.
KNAPP, GIDEON L.
KINGSLAND, DANIEL C.
KINGSLAND, AMBROSE C.
KNOX, JOHN M.
KINGSLAND, WILLIAM M.
KEMBLE, GOUVERNEUR.
KINGSLAND, AMBROSE C., JR.

KINGSLAND, GEORGE L.
KETELTAS, HENRY.
KIPP, WILLIAM H.

L

LAWRENCE, JON'N S.
LAWRENCE, FERDINAND.
LUFF, CHARLES E.
LEE, WILLIAM P.
LANE, P. VANZANDT.
LANE, SMITH E.
LAWRENCE, AB'M R., JR.
LOCKWOOD, JOHN B.
LEVERIDGE, BENJAMIN C.

M

MURRAY, JOHN R.
MOUNT, RICHARD E., JR.
MURRAY, DAVID C.
MACDONOUGH, AUGS. R.
MYERS, T. BAILEY.
MANY, FRANCIS.
McLEAN, JAMES M.
MONELL, CLAUDIUS L.
McLEAN, GEORGE W.
MORELL, GEORGE W.
MONELL, JOSEPH S.
MATHER, JOHN C.
MULFORD, ROB'T L.
MEAD, CHARLES D.
MELVILLE, ALLAN.
MEEKS, JOSEPH.
MILLS, JOHN CRUGER
MERRIFIELD, RICHARD.
MONELL, AMBROSE.
McMURRAY, HENRY R.
MELVILLE, THOMAS.
MORRIS, JAMES.
MOTT, WILLIAM B.
MERRITT, WM. H.

N

NELSON, GEORGE P.
NORWOOD, CARLISLE.
NORWOOD, CARLISLE, Jr.
NATHAN, GRATZ.

O

OGDEN, JAMES DE PEYSTER.
OAKLEY, EDWARD J.
OAKLEY, E. B.
OAKLEY, HOBART.

P

PINKNEY, JAMES H.
PRYER, JAMES.
PELL, JOHN B.
PHILLIPS, LEWIS W.
PIFFARD, HENRY G.
PLACE, JAMES K.
PLACE, EPHRAIM B.
PLATT, JOHN H.
PARMELE, T. W.
PECK, WILLIAM J.
POST, SAM'L L., Jr.
PURDY, JACOB HARSEN.
PELL, JOHN H.

Q

QUACKENBOSS, HENRY.

R

ROOME, WALTER.
RHINELANDER, WM. C.
ROGERS, GEORGE P.
REED, ISAAC H.
ROOSEVELT, CORN'S V. S.
ROOSEVELT, JAMES J.
RUTHERFURD, LEWIS M.
REMSEN, WILLIAM.
ROOME, CHARLES.
ROOSEVELT, JAMES A.

REMSEN, ROBERT G.
RICH, JAMES V.
ROOSEVELT, SAMUEL.
REMSEN, HENRY R.
ROMAINE, WORTHINGTON.
ROOSEVELT, HENRY L.
RIDABOCK, JAMES H.
RENWICK, EDWARD S.
ROOSEVELT, THEODORE.
ROOSEVELT ROBERT B.
RIDLEY, JEREMIAH M.
ROGERS, JONES.
RIDABOCK, FRED'K A.
REMSEN, PHŒNIX.

S

STUYVESANT, NICH. W.
SCHERMERHORN, JOHN.
SUYDAM, JOHN R.
SUYDAM, PETER M.
SWORDS, CHARLES R.
SUYDAM, DAVID L.
SLOSSON EDWARD.
SKIDDY, FRANCIS.
SKIDMORE, SAMUEL T.
SMITH, URIAH J.
STRONG, CHARLES E.
SCHELL, AUGUSTUS.
SLOSSON, JOHN.
STORM, THOMAS.
STEWARD, JOHN.
SMIDT, JOHN C. T.
SUYDAM, RICHARD L.
SWORDS, JOHN E.
SWORDS, GEORGE H.
SCHELL, RICHARD.
STANSBURY, EDWARD A.
SMITH, MORGAN L.
SHERWOOD, JOHN H.
SCHELL, EDWARD.
SCUDDER, HENRY J.

SMYTHE, HENRY A.
STUYVESANT A. V. H.
STUYVESANT ROBERT R.
SWAN, BENJ'N L.
SCHUCHARDT F. GEBHARD.
SEWARD, CLARENCE A.
SWART, JOEL N.
SEYMOUR, WM., JR.
SCUDDER, HEWLETT.
SAVAGE, GEORGE W.
SMITH, CHARLES D.
SCHUYLER, PHILIP.
SWARTWOUT, SATTERLEE.
SATTERLEE, EDWARD R.
SCHIEFFELIN, GEORGE R.
STUYVESANT, ROBERT.
SHRADY, WILLIAM.
SHRADY, JACOB.
STOUT, FRANCIS A.
SCOTT, WILLIAM.
SCHIEFFELIN. CHAS. M.
SWAN, WILLIAM L.
SCHENCK, NOAH HUNT.
SCHMELZEL, GEORGE J.

T

TISDALE, JOHN H.
TITUS, JAMES H.
TILLOTSON, GOUVERNEUR.
TIEMANN, DANIEL F.
TUCKER, GIDEON J.
TIMPSON, JAMES A.
THORNE, JOHN W.

V

VERPLANCK, GULIAN C.
VERMILYE, THOMAS E.
VERMILYE, WILLIAM M.
VERMILYE, WASHINGTON R.
VERMILYE, THOMAS E., JR.
VERMILYE, ROBERT M.
VERMILYE, WILLIAM E.
VAN WINKLE, EDGAR S.

VANDERPOEL, AARON.
VAN DUZER, SELAH.
VAN NORDEN, JAMES.
VANOLINDA, AARON B.
VAN BEUREN, MICHAEL M.
VAN DUZER, ARCHIBALD S.
VAN WINKLE, ISAAC.
VAN SANTVOORD, CORNELIUS.
VAN NOSTRAND, DAVID.
VERMILYE, JACOB D.
VAN VLIET, STEWART.
VOSBURGH, BENJ. F.
VAN SCHAICK, JENKINS.
VANDERPOEL, AARON J.

W

WARNER, ANDREW.
WINTHROP, HENRY R.
WAGSTAFF, DAVID.
WARREN, JOHN.
WARNER, PETER R.
WINTHROP, THOMAS C.
WESTERVELT, JACOB A.
WOLFE, JOHN.
WEMPLE, CHRISTOPHER Y.
WARD, SYLVESTER L. H.
WOOD, JAMES R.
WATERS, GEORGE G.
WOOD, J. WARDELL.
WISNER, WILLIAM H.
WILLIAMS, GEORGE H.
WILLIS, EDWARD.
WELLS, JAMES N.
WILLIS, WILLIAM H., JR.
WILLIS, FRANCIS.
WEMPLE, HENRY Y.
WARD, EGBERT
WETMORE, THEODORE R.
WINTHROP, EGERTON L.
WALLIS, ALEXANDER H.

Y

YATES, CHARLES.

List of Former Members,

Who, by death, resignation or othe.wise, since the organization of the Society, have ceased to be Members.

A

Arthur, Edward H.
Addoms, Charles.
Asten, Abraham.
Anderson, Smith W.
Anderson, Abel T.
Anderson, Henry J.
Andariese, Edward.
Anthony, Jacob.
Adams, William.
Adams, William.
Adriance, Isaac.
Astor, William B.
Anthony, Richard K.
Ashfield, Alfred.
Anderson, C. Van Allen.
Alstyne, John.

B

Bleecker, Anthony J.
Beebee, George W.
Bunker, William I.
Bogert, Peter J.
Bristed, Charles A.
Breese, William G.
Browne, James E.
Bloodgood, Abraham.
Benson, Robert.
Brinckerhoff, James L.
Benson, Egbert.
Beck, John B.
Brinckerhoff, Elbert A.
Bogert, Cornelius R.
Beeckman, John H.
Bronson, Arthur.
Bloodgood, Nathaniel.
Bibby, Edward W.

Bayard, Robert.
Beckman, John K.
Bogardus, Robert.
Brinckerhoff, Peter R.
Beeckman, Henry.
Brevoort, Henry.
Brouwer, John.
Bowne, Samuel.
Bogart, Eugene.
Brady, Henry Austin.
Bleecker, Anthony L.
Bleecker, Garrat N.
Boyd, John J.
Berrian, William, D.D.
Browne, George W.
Brewer, Merwin R.
Banker, Edward.

C

Crosby, William H.
Cruger, Henry D.
Crane, John J.
Cotheal, Isaac E.
Cruger, William E.
Clark, Lewis G.
Coleman, Robert B.
Cooper, Peter.
Campbell, James.
Creighton, William.
Colden, David C.
Cornell, George J.
Clinton, Charles A.
Chardavoyne, William.
Campbell, Duncan P.
Codwise, David.
Crane, Theodore.
Crane, Benjamin F.
Carow, Isaac.

Campbell, John D.
Cebra, John Y.
Chrystie, Thomas W.
Clute, John D.
Campbell, A. Post.
Coles, Isaac U
Chadwick, William N.
Crosby, John P.
Clark, Hull.
Cheesman, John C.
Chambers, James.
Cooper, James S.
Crosby, William B.
Clark, Edwin.
Cotheal, Henry L.

D

Douglas, William.
Drake, Elias G.
Dibblee, William W.
De Lamater, Charles H.
Duer, William A.
Dash, Daniel B.
Duer, John
Duer. George W.
Dean, Nicholas.
De Kay, James E.
Dunscomb, William E.
Davis, George.
Dodge, William.
De Peyster, Pierre C.
Delaplaine, John F.
De Peyster, Arent S.
Delafield, John.
De Peyster, Robert G. L.
Dederer, Charles.
De Kay, George C.
Deas, Fitz Allen.
De Witt, Thomas.
Dayton, William G.
Duer, Denning.
Dumont, William.
De Peyster, William.
De Motte, Mortimer.
Dean, Edmund F.
De Peyster, Nicholas.
Dusenberry, W. Coxe.
Davis, Gilbert.

Dash, Daniel B.

E

Embury, Peter.
Edgar, William.
Edgar, Newbold.
Embury, Philip A.
Edmonds, Francis W.
Embury, Daniel, Jr.

F

Francis, Henry M.
Francis, John W.
Finlay, J. Beekman.
Fowler, Theodosius A.
Fraser, Donald.
Fink, Charles.
Fowler, Isaac V.
Fardon, Abraham, Jr
Fardon, Abraham, Sr.
Fleming, Augustus.
Funck, James.
Forrester, James C
Fardon, William.

G

Goodhue, Robert C.
Gilford, Samuel, Jr.
Garr, Andrew S.
Graham, Charles.
Giles, George W.
Goelet, Peter.
Glover, Samuel.
Gouverneur, Samuel L.
Greenfield, John V.
Giraud, Jacob P.
Giraud, Daniel.
Groshon, John.
Gerry, Elbridge, Sr.

H

Hunter, Wm. A.
Heyer, Cornelius.
Hobart, William H.
Hoffman, Ogden.
Hone, Philip.
Hone, Isaac S.
Hosack, David.
Hoffman, Richard K.

Heyer, Henry A.
Heyer, Edward P.
Hosack, Alexander E.
Hoffman, George E.
Hoffman, Lindley M.
Halsey, Anthony P.
Hawkes, W. Wright.
Hicks, Silas, Jr.
Hamersley, Andrew S.
Heiser, Christopher.
Hunter, Abraham T.
Hoffman, Charles F.
Hamilton, James A.
Haight, Benjamin.
Hoffman, Martin.
Hamersley, Lewis C.
Hackett, James H.
Hone, Robert S.
Hallett, William P.
Halsted, Jonathan.
Haight, George.
Henry, Philip.
Hammond, Charles H.
Haight, John E.
Hull, Oliver.
Hardenbrook, John K.
Hobart, Dayton.
Harsen, Jacob.
Henry, John T.
Haws, Robert T.

I

Irving, Washington.
Irving, Ebenezer.
Irving, John T.
Irving, Gabriel F.

J

Johnston, John.
Johnson, Jeromus.
Jones, James I.
Jones, Edward R.
Jones, John.
Jones, Isaac, Jr.
Johnson, James C.
Jones, David S.
Jay, Peter Augustus.

Jones, Samuel.
Johnson, William.
Jones, William G.
Judah, S. B. Helbert.
Johnson, Wm T.
Jacobson, Fred'k.

K

King, James G.
Kermit, Robert.
Keese, John D.
Kearney, Philip J.
Kip, James H.
Keese, John.
Kip, John I.
Kissam, Richard S.
Kemble, Richard F.
Knevels, Delancy W.
King, Charles.
King, John A.
Kip, Leonard W.
Kip, Brockholst L.

L

Lawrence, Wiliam A.
Leveridge, John.
Lang, John.
Lott, Henry.
Laight, Edward W.
Leonard, John.
Low, Nicholas.
Le Roy, Daniel.
Le Roy, Herman.
Lawrence, Richard M.
Lawrence, John L.
Lorillard, Jacob.
Laight, William E.
Lawrence, William B.
Lefferts, James.
Lee, James.
Lownds, Oliver M.
Ludlow, Edward G.
Lownds, James M.
Low, Cornelius.
Le Roy, Herman, Jr.
Livingston, John W.
Lott, Jerome.

Luqueer, Francis S.
Leveridge, Benjamin C.
Labagh, John I.
Low, J. Augustus.
Leconte, John L.
Le Roy, Jacob R.
Lee, Benjamin C.
Lawrence, Abraham R.
Le Roy, Jacob.
Lossing, Benson J.

M

Manley, James R.
Mercein, Thomas R.
McCartee, Robert.
McKnight, J. M. Scott.
McEvers, Bache.
McEvers, Charles, Jr.
McLean, Hugh.
Maxwell, William H.
Murray, John R.
Morris, William Lewis.
Morse, Samuel F. B.
Main, Austin L. S.
Mandeville, William.
Mulligan John W.
McCullough, James.
Milledoler, Philip E.
Miller, Sylvanus.
Moore, Boltis.
Many, Francis V.
Mott, John G.
Morris, Robert H.
Mesier, Edward S.
Mapes, James J.
Morris, Richard L.
Manley, James.
McCoun, William T.
McVickar, Benjamin.
Minturn, Robert B.
McFarlan, Francis.
Morford, Charles A.
Mitchill, George.

N

Neilson, John, Jr.
Neilson, Anthony B.

Nathan, Jonathan.
Nicoll, Edward A.
Nathan, Benjamin.
Nathan, Seixas.
Neill, Samuel M.
Nichols, Robert.
Nicoll, Henry.
Nicoll, Solomon T.
Nesbitt, Geo. F.
Nevius, Jacob R.

O

Oothout, John.
Onderdonk, Benjamin T.
Oakley, Charles.
Ogden, Richard H.
Ogsbury, Francis.
Oakley, Cornelius.
Oothout, William.
Ogden, Nicholas G.
Ogden, John D.

P

Paulding, James K.
Paterson, Matthew C.
Paulding, William.
Phœnix, Daniel A.
Pierson, Henry L.
Pell, Alfred.
Patterson, John M.
Pell, Duncan C.
Parshall, Charles.
Popham, Charles W.
Phœnix, J. Phillips.
Pryer, John.
Phyfe, James D.
Post, Waldron B.
Prime, Frederick.
Prime, Rufus.
Pierrepont, Henry E.
Penfold, Edmund.

Q

Quackenbos, Nicholas.
Quackenbos, Mangle M.

R

Ruckel, Philip P.
Rapelye, George B.
Ray, Richard.
Rapelje, George.
Robinson, Beverley.
Romaine, Samuel B.
Romaine, Benjamin.
Raymond, Samuel G.
Rhinelander, John R.
Rogers, John.
Rodgers, J. Kearney.
Rice, Thomas D.
Roberts, Marshall O.
Robinson, William D.
Robinson, Henry.
Ray, Robert.
Renwick, James.
Ridley, John.
Rockwell, William.
Richards, Benj., Jr.
Roosevelt, Chas. H.

S

Stuyvesant, Peter G.
Schermerhorn, Peter.
Schermerhorn, Edmund H.
Schermerhorn, Abraham.
Smith, George B.
Schermerhorn, Archibald B.
Schermerhorn, John P.
Schermerhorn, John S
Schermerhorn, Peter A.
Schermerhorn, Peter B.
Strong, James.
Stuyvesant, Peter.
Strong, George W.
Strong, George T.
Stagg, John T.
Stagg, Benjamin.
Stagg, Benjamin, Jr.
Schermerhorn, John J.
Simonson, John.
Swartwout, Samuel.
Stagg, Peter.
Stevens, Robert L.
Sanford, Edward.
Stuyvesant, Gerard.

Skellorn, George W.
Smith, Thomas R.
Schermerhorn, A. Van Cortlandt.
Schermerhorn, J. Lefferts.
Seixas, Jacob B.
Sidell, William H.
Slipper, Henry U.
Suydam, Lambert.
Stagg, Gerard S.
Smith, Fletcher.
Stewart, James J.
Stout, Aquila G.
Swords, James R.
Swords, Edward J.
Storm, Garrit.
Stoutenburgh, William E.
Seton, Alfred.
Strong, P. Remsen.
Smith, Cornelius.
Stagg, Junius T.
Stevens, Alexander H.
Sutphen, John.
Seaman, John F.
Striker, Garret H.
Seymour, Daniel.
Striker, Garret H., Jr.
Staples, William J.
Schoonmaker, Henry.
Storm, John G.
Smith, Edwin.
Sherman, Watts.
Schermerhorn, Chas A.
Smith, Washington.
Suydam. James A.
Schmelzel, George.
Schmelzel, John B.

T

Tylee, Daniel E.
Turner, John.
Titus, Peter S.
Turner, William.
Thomas, James P.
Tucker, Fanning C.
Townsend, Isaac.
Turk, William.
Tompkins, Minthorne.

Tompkins, Ray.
Thompson, Alexander B.
Thorne, John M.
Townsend, John J.
Tillou, Francis R.
Tappan, Henry P.
Talman, George F.
Townsend, Effingham L.

V

Van Buren, Martin.
Varick, Abraham.
Varick, Richard.
Van Wagenen, William I.
Verplanck, William W.
Van Wagenen, Hubert.
Van Wagenen, Garret G.
Van Nest, Abraham.
Vandervoort, Peter L.
Van Antwerp, William.
Verplanck, Samuel.
Van Wyck, William.
Van Wagenen, William W.
Van Zandt, Peter P.
Van Nostrand, James.
Van Benschoten, James.
Van Antwerp, James.
Van Nostrand, Jacob.
Van Wyck, Charles.
Van Wagenen, George A.
Vandervoort, James.
Vandervoort, John L.
Van Wagenen, Frederic.
Van Duzer, William A. S
Van Buren, John.
Vandervoort, Charles.
Vandervoort, Peter II.
Van Buren, John D.
Valentine, David T.
Vanderpoel, Jesse O.
Vanderpoel, John.

W

Wyckoff, Alexander R.
Wenman, Evert.
Wyckoff, Henry I.
Wilkes, George.
Wynkoop, Augustus.
Walker, John W.
Wilkins, Gouverneur M.
Westervelt, Harman.
Watts, John.
Willis, Oliver W.
Wolfe, Christopher.
Wright, Henry A.
Westervelt, Harman C.
Westervelt, Isaac Y.
Ward, Theodore A.
Wyckoff, Henry S.
Wyckoff, Henry.
Waldron, Victor B.
Webb, J. Watson.
Ward, Richard R.
Wilson, William.
Walsh, Alexander R.
Ward, Samuel, Jr.
Wilmerding, William E.
Waddell, William C. H.
Walsh, James W.
Walton, Edward H.
Winthrop, Benj. R.
Wessells, Francis.
Westervelt, John S.
Ward, Moses.
Wessells, Wessell.
Ward, Augustus H.
Willis, William II.

Z

Zabriskie, Albert G.
Zabriskie, Martin R.

www.ingramcontent.com/pod-product-compliance
Lightning Source LLC
Chambersburg PA
CBHW021634270326
41931CB00008B/1013